Biostatis[...]
by Example
Using SAS® Studio

Ron Cody

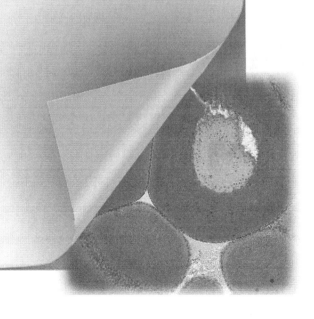

support.sas.com/bookstore

C000153353

The correct bibliographic citation for this manual is as follows: Cody, Ron. 2016. *Biostatistics by Example Using SAS® Studio*. Cary, NC: SAS Institute Inc.

Biostatistics by Example Using SAS® Studio

Copyright © 2016, SAS Institute Inc., Cary, NC, USA

ISBN 978-1-62960-328-5 (Hard copy)
ISBN 978-1-62960-493-0 (EPUB)
ISBN 978-1-62960-494-7 (MOBI)
ISBN 978-1-62960-495-4 (PDF)

All Rights Reserved. Produced in the United States of America.

For a hard copy book: No part of this publication may be reproduced, stored in a retrieval system, or transmitted, in any form or by any means, electronic, mechanical, photocopying, or otherwise, without the prior written permission of the publisher, SAS Institute Inc.

For a web download or e-book: Your use of this publication shall be governed by the terms established by the vendor at the time you acquire this publication.

The scanning, uploading, and distribution of this book via the Internet or any other means without the permission of the publisher is illegal and punishable by law. Please purchase only authorized electronic editions and do not participate in or encourage electronic piracy of copyrighted materials. Your support of others' rights is appreciated.

U.S. Government License Rights; Restricted Rights: The Software and its documentation is commercial computer software developed at private expense and is provided with RESTRICTED RIGHTS to the United States Government. Use, duplication, or disclosure of the Software by the United States Government is subject to the license terms of this Agreement pursuant to, as applicable, FAR 12.212, DFAR 227.7202-1(a), DFAR 227.7202-3(a), and DFAR 227.7202-4, and, to the extent required under U.S. federal law, the minimum restricted rights as set out in FAR 52.227-19 (DEC 2007). If FAR 52.227-19 is applicable, this provision serves as notice under clause (c) thereof and no other notice is required to be affixed to the Software or documentation. The Government's rights in Software and documentation shall be only those set forth in this Agreement.

SAS Institute Inc., SAS Campus Drive, Cary, NC 27513-2414

September 2016

SAS® and all other SAS Institute Inc. product or service names are registered trademarks or trademarks of SAS Institute Inc. in the USA and other countries. ® indicates USA registration.

Other brand and product names are trademarks of their respective companies.

SAS software may be provided with certain third-party software, including but not limited to open-source software, which is licensed under its applicable third-party software license agreement. For license information about third-party software distributed with SAS software, refer to **http://support.sas.com/thirdpartylicenses**.

Contents

About This Book

Purpose

SAS University Edition and its user interface, SAS Studio, have become very popular. SAS Studio can also be used with standard versions of SAS, perhaps as an alternative to SAS Enterprise Guide. SAS Studio includes built-in tasks for importing data from external files (Excel, for example) and, best of all, it includes point-and-click statistical tasks for just about any statistical study. This book will benefit the reader by doing the following:

1. Providing step-by-step instructions, complete with screen shots, of how to use SAS University Edition and SAS Studio to perform most statistical queries.

2. Discussing the theory behind each statistical test, with emphasis on the assumptions that need to be satisfied before running each test.

3. Helping the reader negotiate some of the trickier aspects of running SAS University Edition. For example, this book explains how to access files on a local hard drive and make them available on the virtual machine where SAS is running.

4. Providing a detailed explanation of the output produced by each statistical procedure.

5. Presenting practice problems (with solutions to the odd-numbered problems).

Is This Book for You?

The audience for this book consists mostly of students in a statistics or a biostatistics class. Although the book uses biostatistical examples, students in other classes such as educational or business statistics will also benefit. In addition, data analysts in the pharmaceutical industry will also find valuable information in this book.

Prerequisites

There is NO prerequisite for readers of this book. It is written with the assumption that the reader has never used SAS before.

Scope of This Book

The first section of this book explains how to install the SAS University Edition and the virtualization software needed to run it. Readers of this book may also be using SAS Studio with a standard edition of SAS (as opposed to the SAS University Edition).

Subsequent chapters describe how to import data from a variety of sources such as Excel workbooks and CSV files.

Following these chapters is a chapter on using the SAS Studio tasks to perform descriptive statistics, the first step in almost any data analysis project.

Most of the remaining chapters cover all the basic statistical tests commonly used in biostatistical analysis.

A final chapter is devoted to sample size and power calculations. This topic is not usually covered in a book of this type, even though it is a very important topic.

After reading this book, you will be able to understand temporary and permanent SAS data sets and how to create them from various data sources. The reader will also be able to use SAS Studio Statistics tasks to generate descriptive statistics for continuous and categorical data.

The inferential statistics portion of the book covers the following:

- Paired and unpaired *t* tests

- One-way analysis of variance

- N-Way ANOVA

- Correlation

- Simple and multiple regression

- Logistic regression

- Categorical data analysis

- Power and sample size calculations

About the Examples

Software Used to Develop the Book's Content

All of the statistical tasks described and demonstrated in this book are available to anyone using SAS Studio, either as part of SAS University Edition or as an interface to standard versions of SAS.

SAS University Edition

If you are using SAS University Edition, you can use the code and data sets provided with this book. This helpful link will get you started: http://support.sas.com/publishing/import_ue.data.html.

Exercise Solutions

Each chapter, starting with Chapter 3, includes a set of problems for the reader to test his or her skills. Solutions to the odd-numbered problems are included in the book—solutions to the even-numbered problems are available from SAS Institute, on request.

Additional Help

Although this book illustrates many analyses regularly performed in businesses across industries, questions specific to your aims and issues may arise. To fully support you, SAS Institute and SAS Press offer you the following help resources:

- For questions about topics covered in this book, contact the author through SAS Press:
  - Send questions by email to saspress@sas.com; include the book title in your correspondence.
  - Submit feedback on the author's page at http://support.sas.com/publishing/bbu/companion_site/info.html.
- For questions about topics in or beyond the scope of this book, post queries to the relevant SAS Support Communities at https://communities.sas.com/.
- SAS Institute maintains a comprehensive website with up-to-date information. One page that is particularly useful to both the novice and the seasoned SAS user is its Knowledge Base. Search for relevant notes in the "Samples and SAS Notes" section of the Knowledge Base at http://support.sas.com/resources.
- Registered SAS users or their organizations can access SAS Customer Support at http://support.sas.com. Here you can pose specific questions to SAS Customer Support; under *Support*, click *Submit a Problem*. You will need to provide an email address to which replies can be sent, identify your organization, and provide a customer site number or license information. This information can be found in your SAS logs.

Keep in Touch

We look forward to hearing from you. We invite questions, comments, and concerns. If you want to contact us about a specific book, please include the book title in your correspondence.

Contact the Author through SAS Press

- By email: saspress@sas.com
- Via the web: http://support.sas.com/publishing/bbu/companion_site/info.html

Purchase SAS Books

For a complete list of books available through SAS, visit sas.com/store/books.

- Phone: 1-800-727-0025
- Email: sasbook@sas.com

Subscribe to the SAS Learning Report

Receive up-to-date information about SAS training, certification, and publications via email by subscribing to the SAS Learning Report monthly eNewsletter. Read the archives and subscribe today at http://support.sas.com/community/newsletters/training!

Publish with SAS

SAS is recruiting authors! Are you interested in writing a book? Visit http://support.sas.com/publishing/publish/index.html for more information.

About The Author

 Ron Cody, EdD, a retired professor from the Robert Wood Johnson Medical School now works as a private consultant and a national instructor for SAS Institute Inc. A SAS user since 1977, Ron's extensive knowledge and innovative style have made him a popular presenter at local, regional, and national SAS conferences. He has authored or co-authored numerous books, including *Learning SAS by Example: A Programmer's Guide*, and, *An Introduction to SAS University Edition*; as well as countless articles in medical and scientific journals.

"Ron and Mickey" photo by Jan Cody

Learn more about this author by visiting Ron Cody's author page at http://support.sas.com/publishing/authors/cody.html. There you can download free book excerpts, access example code and data, read the latest reviews, get updates, and more.

Acknowledgments

This is the fun part. I'm mostly finished writing (just need to check the review copy), and I can now sit down and take the time to thank the small community that helped me put this book together.

I was delighted to have Sian Roberts once again as the acquisition and developmental editor. She really gets things done—and quickly! This is the third book that I have written under her guidance. Thanks, Sian.

Next, I would like to give a shout-out to my reviewers. Jeff Smith (professor and associate dean at the University of Otago, New Zealand, also of Cody and Smith fame), Gerry Hobbs (professor of Statistics at West Virginia University), and Marc Huber (statistics instructor for SAS) were especially helpful in ensuring that I didn't make any technical errors in my statistical discussions. Paul Grant has reviewed almost all of my books and keeps coming back for more! His attention to detail and in-depth knowledge of SAS were an invaluable asset. Finally, Amy Peters was my go-to person for all questions related to the SAS University Edition and SAS Studio. She is a delight to work with.

One of the most important jobs in publishing a book that reads well and is mostly error free is done by the copy editor. I was delighted to have Kathy Underwood take on this task.

There has to be someone who puts everything together. That job went to Denise Jones. Her title is technical publishing specialist but that doesn't really tell the story. She is the person who converted the "pieces parts" into a coherent book.

Robert Harris produced the cover for my last book (Introduction to SAS University Edition) and has once again produced a cover that really pops. Thanks, Robert.

Chapter 1: What Is the SAS University Edition?

Introduction

Many of you will be accessing SAS Studio along with the SAS University edition. If you are using SAS Studio with an edition of SAS that is not the SAS University Edition, you can skip right to Chapter 2 to see how you can use SAS Studio to manage and report your data, to create graphs and reports, and to perform most of the statistical tasks performed by biostatisticians. The examples in this book all use the SAS University Edition, but users of SAS Studio in other environments will see that the statistical tasks are identical to the ones described here.

SAS University Edition is a full version of SAS software that is free to anyone, and it runs on Microsoft Windows computers as well as Apple laptops and Linux workstations. How can this be?

When you download this free software, you agree that you will not use it for commercial purposes. As a student or researcher using the SAS University Edition to learn how SAS works, this is not a problem. Once you have mastered the statistical and other tasks using SAS University Edition, you can use those same skills with the licensed versions of SAS used by universities and in the corporate world.

A huge advantage of using the SAS University Edition is that you access SAS using an interface called SAS Studio. This provides a programming environment that allows you to write SAS programs, but, more importantly, provides you with an interactive point-and-click interface where you can quickly and easily run a large variety of statistical tests.

This looks too good to be true. Well, there is a slight complication that results from allowing SAS University Edition to run on PCs, Apple, and Linux computers—that is, after you download the SAS University software, you also need to download and install something called virtualization software. If you are not familiar with this term, you are not alone. This author was a complete novice using virtualization software when the first book, *An Introduction to SAS University Edition*, was written. Since then, especially with the help of my younger son, I am much more comfortable with these tools.

A virtual computer is a computer that runs on your real computer, running its own operating system and accessing files on your real computer (this is the tricky part). In the PC (Windows) environment, you have several choices of virtualization software. SAS is now recommending a product called Oracle VM VirtualBox. You can download this for free for your own use. This is an "open source" product that is supported by Oracle Systems and it supports all of the operating systems mentioned. The other alternative for Windows and Linux is called VMware Workstation Player (formally, just called VMware Player). This is still free for non-commercial use. For Apple products, you can also run VMware Fusion (there is a fee).

Because SAS is now recommending VirtualBox for PC users, the screen shots in this book will use that product. This author has installed both VirtualBox and VMware Player and determined that once you enter the SAS Studio environment, you cannot tell the difference. The bottom line is that once you install one of the virtualization tools, all of the tasks and SAS programs will run exactly the same.

How to Download the SAS University Edition

Many of you, this author included, often feel a bit nervous when downloading and installing new software. If you are in this group (probably a bit older like me), find a younger, tech-savvy person to look over your shoulder.

To obtain your free copy of the SAS University Edition, use the following URL:

http://www.sas.com/en_us/software/university-edition.html

This brings up the following screen (Figure 1):

Figure 1: Obtaining SAS University Edition

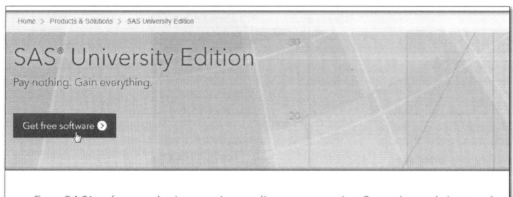

Click the box labeled "Get free software" to bring up the next screen (Figure 2).

From here on, if you see the word "click," assume it means left-click. Any time a right-click is required, it will be specified.

Figure 2: Next Step in Obtaining SAS University Edition

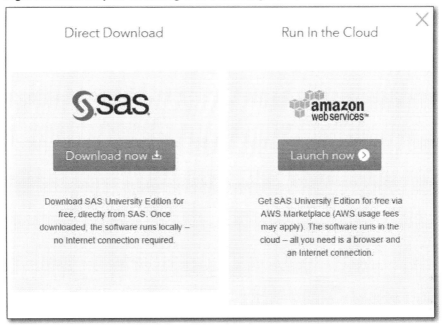

Click Download now (unless you plan to use Amazon Web Services – AWS). This brings up the following screen:

Figure 3: SAS Download Screen

Figure 3 shows the required configuration for a Windows machine. If you click OS X, you will see a different list of requirements (Figure 4):

Figure 4: Requirements for OS X

If you have an older machine (for example, a PC running a 32-bit operating system), you can search the virtualization sites for older versions that will be compatible with your computer.

Once you are satisfied, that your computer meets the requirements for running one of the virtualization software applications, scroll down to the choice of virtualization software that you want to install. In Figure 5, you are choosing VirtualBox.

Figure 5: Choose your Virtualization Software

Once you have downloaded the virtualization software, click on one of the links farther down on the screen, download a PDF or watch a video (or both) giving you detailed instructions how to set up your virtualization software and SAS Studio.

Figure 6: Obtain the Get Started Guides (PDF or Videos)

Get the Quick Start Guide (PDF or Video).

And don't just download the PDF – actually read it. Or watch the video if that's more your thing. Or do both!

Quick Start PDF

Download PDF

Seriously. The Quick Start Guides give you step-by-step instructions for installing and configuring SAS University Edition on your laptop or desktop computer. You won't regret it.

Quick Start Video

Watch video

Finally, you are ready to download the appropriate version of SAS University Edition (Figure 7):

Figure 7: Download Appropriate Version of SAS University Edition

If you followed the instructions in the appropriate PDF or video, you will have set up a folder on your computer called \SASUniversityEdition\myfolders. This is the location where SAS University Edition can automatically find files on your hard drive. If you want to access files in other folders on your hard drive, you will need to set up shared folders. (This will be explained in Chapter 3 for those who are interested or need to access data from different locations on their hard drive.) For learning purposes, it is best to place all your data files in SASUniversityEdition\myfolders directory.

Conclusions

Yes, there is a bit of work (some of it scary) to set up and run the SAS University Edition on your computer. However, there are many sources of help if you have trouble. And you only have to do it once!

The next few chapters discuss some of the built-in data sets that you can use to perfect your skills, as well as instructions for using your own data, either on Excel spreadsheets (a very common data source) or text files.

Chapter 2: SAS Studio Tasks

Introduction

Hopefully, you have installed your visualization software and the SAS University Edition (or you are running SAS Studio with a standard version of SAS). Now, it's time to get started. You start your virtual computer by double-clicking on the appropriate icon on your desktop (the installation process should have placed this icon there). If you don't see an icon for VirtualBox or one of the versions of VMware, you need to browse through your program list and create a shortcut on your desktop.

As an example, here is what you will see if you open VirtualBox:

Figure 1: Opening VirtualBox

Your screen may look a bit different. Double-click SAS University Edition.

A window will pop up that looks like this:

Figure 2: Opening SAS University Edition (VirtualBox)

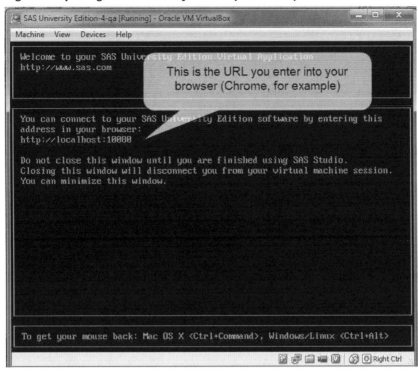

The URL may be different from this. Once you enter it into your browser, you will want to bookmark it so that you don't have to type it every time you want to run the SAS University Edition. If you use a version of VMware, the URL will look something like an IP address such as

http://192.168.117.129

Regardless of which virtualization software you use, you will be directed to the SAS University Edition: Information Center screen. It looks like this:

Figure 3: Opening Screen of SAS University Edition: Information Center

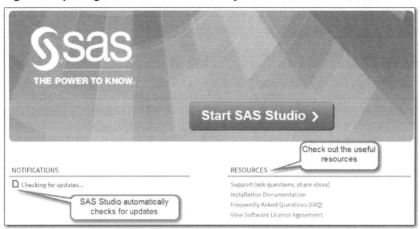

If you see a message telling you that updates are available, you can click the Update icon or click the Start SAS Studio button and update at some other time. The Resources link is also very valuable—you can access help files, videos, books (even some of mine), and the always popular FAQs (frequently asked questions).

Using the Built-in Tasks

To open SAS Studio, click "Start SAS Studio."

Figure 4: Opening Screen for SAS Studio

As you can see in Figure 4, the rectangle on the left is called the navigation pane and the larger rectangular area on the right is called the work area. The navigation pane, as the name implies, allows you to select tasks, browse files and folders, import data from a variety of sources such as Excel workbooks, and do other useful tasks that you will see a bit later.

The work area consists of three sub-areas called Code, Log, and Results. You can switch to any one of these areas by clicking on the appropriate tab. This is what you see if you are in SAS Programmer mode. You see different tabs when you are in Visual Programmer mode. We will stick to SAS Programmer Mode for all the examples in this book.

The Code section is where you can write SAS programs (also the place where SAS Studio writes programs for you). The Log area displays information about data being read or written, syntax errors in your SAS code, and information on how much CPU time and total time were used to run your program. The Results area is where SAS Studio displays the tables, graphs, and statistics that either you programmed yourself or you had one or more of the built-in SAS Studio tasks produce for you.

Taking a Tour of the Navigation Pane

Figure 5 is an enlargement of the navigation pane.

Figure 5: Enlarged View of the Navigation Pane

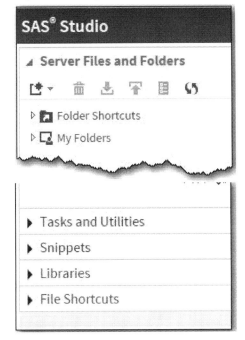

When you click on any of the choices in the navigation pane, it expands and moves higher in the list. You can also expand or contract any of the sub-lists by clicking on the triangles to the left of the choices.

Exploring the LIBRARIES Tab

Let's start your exploration of SAS Studio by clicking the Libraries tab. Your Navigation pane will now look something like this:

Figure 6: SAS Libraries

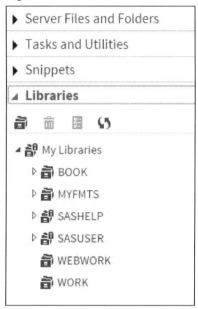

Notice that the triangle to the left of the word Libraries is now pointing downward, telling you that you are looking at sub-lists. Under My Libraries, you see a list of libraries. Libraries are places where SAS puts programs and data sets (think of folders on your hard drive). This author has already created two libraries (BOOK and MYFMTS), so you will not see those libraries on your computer. However, SAS Studio comes with some libraries already installed. The WORK library is a temporary library—all data and programs placed there will not be automatically saved when you exit SAS Studio.

The SASHELP library contains over 200 data sets, covering a variety of topics such as car sales and health data. These data sets are quite useful because you can use them for examples or testing your code. Click the SASHELP library to see the list of built-in data sets (see Figure 7 below):

Figure 7: Expanding the SASHELP Libraries

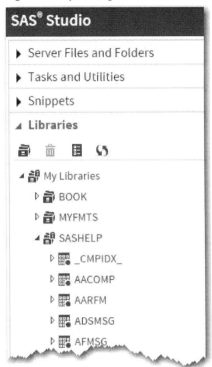

Let's scroll down to the HEART data set to demonstrate some of the features of SAS Studio. You can either double-click the HEART library or highlight it or drag it to the work area. When you do this, SAS Studio displays the columns of the table and a listing of some of the top rows and columns of the actual table.

Note: Throughout this book and in the various SAS Studio tasks, the terms Columns and Variables, Rows and Observations, and data sets and tables are used interchangeably. Originally, SAS used the terms Variables, Observations, and data sets instead of the terminology that came along with many database programs (such as SQL) where the terms Columns, Rows, and tables were used instead.

Having opened the HEART data set, your screen will look as follows:

Figure 8: The HEART Data Set

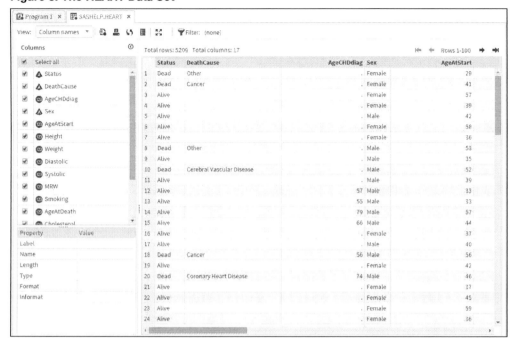

The Columns (variables) in the data set are displayed on the left (Figure 9):

Figure 9: Columns in the HEART Data Set

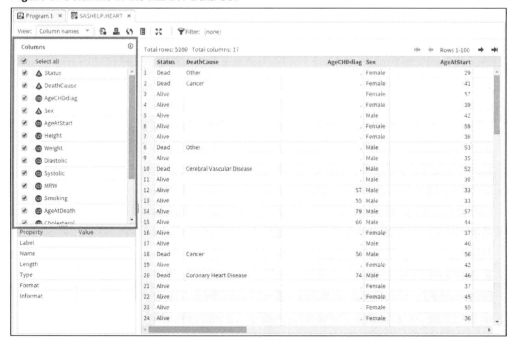

You can click Select all to toggle between selecting all the variables or none. You will see two easy ways to select columns in just a moment.

The right side of the screen shows a portion of the actual table (Figure 10):

Figure 10: Columns and Rows from the HEART Data Set

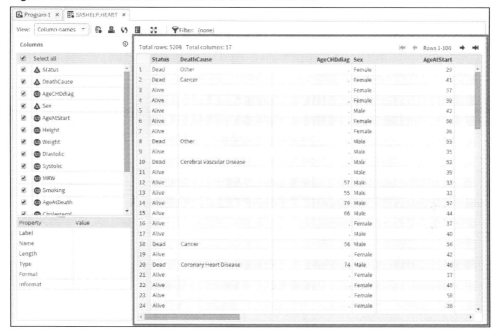

You can use the horizontal and vertical scroll bars to examine additional columns and rows of this table (Figure 11):

Figure 11: Horizontal and Vertical Scroll Bars

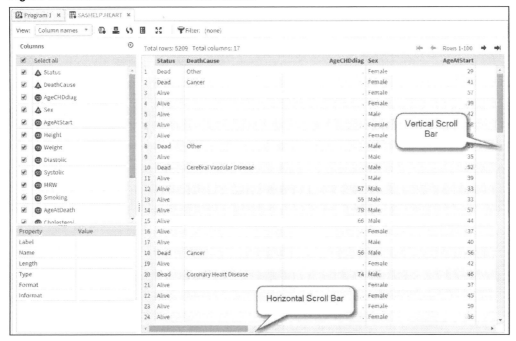

As promised, you will now see how to select (or deselect) columns from a table. If you want to display just a few columns, it is best to click Select all to deselect all of the columns. Then, to select the columns that you want, using one or both of these methods:

1) Click the check box of any column to select it—it will be displayed in the table. If a column is already selected, you can deselect it if you uncheck it.

2) Click the check box of one column, hold down the Shift key and double-click the check box of another column. All columns from the first to the last will be selected.

In Figure 12 (below), columns for Sex, Height, Weight, Diastolic (diastolic blood pressure), and Systolic (systolic blood pressure) were selected.

Figure 12: Selecting Variables

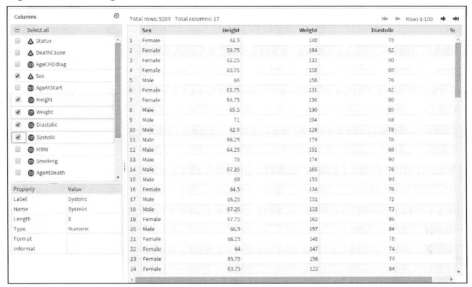

To resize a column, move the cursor to the right side of a column on the top row of the table (where you see the column headings). When the cursor turns into two parallel lines, hold down the left-click on your mouse (or touch pad) and drag the column boundary right or left (see Figure 13 below).

Figure 13: Resizing Columns

Total rows: 5209   Total columns: 17

	Sex	Height	Weight
1	Female	62.5	140
2	Female	59.75	194
3	Female	62.25	132
4	Female	65.75	158
5	Male	66	156
6	Female	61.75	131
7	Female	64.75	136

Moving Columns

To move a column, place the cursor on a column name in the top row. It will change shape and become a hand. For example, if you want to move the column labeled Diastolic, place the cursor on the column heading for Diastolic (Figure 14):

Figure 14: Moving Columns (first step)

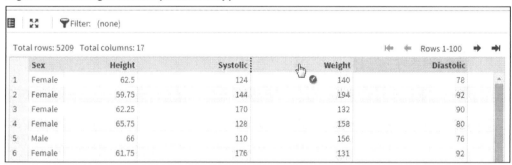

Hold down and left-click the mouse button, drag the column to the desired position, and release the button. For example, if you want Diastolic to be next to Systolic, drag the hand pointer to the column to the right of Systolic (and to the left of the Weight label). (See Figure 15 below):

Figure 15: Moving Columns (second step)

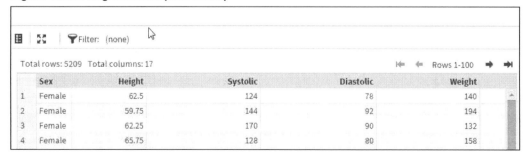

Release the left mouse button and the column is moved. (See Figure 16 below):

Figure 16: Moving Columns (final result)

	Sex	Height	Systolic	Diastolic	Weight
	Filter: (none)				
	Total rows: 5209 Total columns: 17			Rows 1-100	
	Sex	Height	Systolic	Diastolic	Weight
1	Female	62.5	124	78	140
2	Female	59.75	144	92	194
3	Female	62.25	170	90	132
4	Female	65.75	128	80	158

Sorting Columns

There are two ways to sort a column. The first method is to place the cursor on the column heading (as if you were planning to move it) and left-click the mouse. A black triangle will appear, pointing up, to indicate that the column is sorted in ascending (low to high) order. (See Figure 17 below):

Figure 17: Sorting Columns (method 1)

Total rows: 5209   Total columns: 17

	Sex	Height	Systolic ▲
1	Female	66.5	82
2	Female	65.75	86
3	Female	64.5	89
4	Female	65	90
5	Male	66.25	90
6	Female	62.75	90
7	Female	61.25	90
8	Female	58.75	90
9	Female	56.5	90
10	Female	58.5	90
11	Female	67	90

If you repeat this process, a descending sort will be performed (Figure 18):

Figure 18: Descending Sort (method 1)

Total rows: 5209   Total columns: 17

	Sex	Height	Systolic ▼
1	Female	62.75	300
2	Female	62	294
3	Female	61.75	290
4	Female	60	286
5	Female	59.75	280
6	Male	66.5	276
7	Female	63.75	272
8	Female	60.75	270
9	Female	61	260

Each time you left-click on a column heading, the column is re-sorted in the opposite direction that it was before.

You can have more control over the appearance of a column, or even the whole table, if you right-click on a column heading. This causes the following menu to appear:

Figure 19: Sorting, Filtering, and Resizing

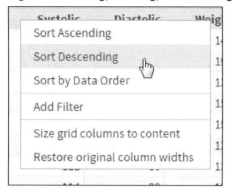

The top two entries provide a second way to sort, either ascending or descending. The third selection, Sort by Data Order, returns the table to its original order. You can Add a Filter to subset rows of the table. If you click the option Size grid columns to content, the column widths will all adjust so that they are the minimum size to hold the values in each column. Using this option is much easier than trying to resize each column manually. The last item in the list restores the column widths to the original size.

As an example of executing some of the right-click options, Figure 20 was produced by executing a descending sort on the column labeled Systolic and sizing grid columns to content.

Figure 20: Descending Sort and Sizing Grid Columns to Content

Total rows: 5209   Total columns: 17

	Sex	Height	Systolic ▼	Diastolic	Weight
1	Female	62.75	300	150	228
2	Female	62	294	144	153
3	Female	61.75	290	124	144
4	Female	60	286	104	204
5	Female	59.75	280	145	189
6	Male	66.5	276	112	186
7	Female	63.75	272	124	115

Filtering a Table (subsetting rows)

You can subset rows in a table by selecting the Filter option shown in Figure 19. Suppose you want to filter the table so that it will contain only rows where Height is greater than 70. First, right-click the column heading Height. Click Add Filter. This brings up a series of conditions (such as equal to, greater than, less than, and so on). Select the operation you want and then enter a value in the text box to the right. In this example, you want to select all rows where Height is greater than 70. You can click the box labeled Filter to complete the task or click the + sign to add other conditions. In this example, you only want the single filter to operate.

Figure 21: Filtering Rows

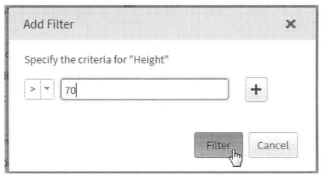

The filtered table is shown in Figure 22 below:

Figure 22: Filtered Table

Total rows: 5209   Total columns: 17   Filtered rows: 402

	Sex	Height	Systolic ▼	Diastolic	Weight
1	Male	70.5	216	126	229
2	Male	72	200	110	227
3	Male	73.5	200	140	178
4	Male	70.5	190	130	226
5	Male	72	190	110	191
6	Male	70.5	188	96	172
7	Male	72.25	180	120	273

If you add multiple filters, either all at once using the + sign to add more filters or right-click on another column and add another filter, the effects are additive. Each filter you create is displayed at the top of the table next to the filter icon (and label). To remove a filter, click the X to the right of any filter to remove it (see Figure 22, below):

Figure 23: Removing a Filter

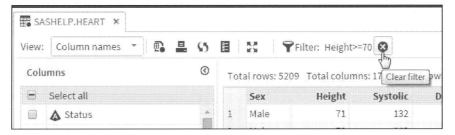

If you create a filter based on a column of character data (see the "A" to the left of the variable name in the list of columns), the filter options show all possible values of the variables and allow you to select one or more values to create your filter.

As an example, suppose you want to see a table containing only female subjects. Right-click the column labeled Sex and click "Female." The table now contains only data for females (see Figure 24 below):

Figure 24: Filtering on a Character Value

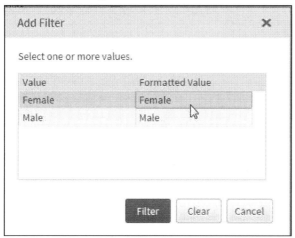

Figure 25: Females Selected

Total rows: 5209   Total columns: 17   Filtered rows: 2873

	Sex	Height	Systolic	Diastolic	Weight
1	Female	62.5	124	78	140
2	Female	59.75	144	92	194
3	Female	62.25	170	90	132
4	Female	65.75	128	80	158
5	Female	61.75	176	92	131
6	Female	64.75	112	80	136

For character columns that have multiple values, you can select several values by one of two methods:

1) Hold down the Control key and click each value you want to include.

2) Click a single value, hold down the Shift key, and click a second value. All values from the first to the second are selected.

You can combine these two method if desired.

Conclusion

In this chapter, you saw how to use built-in SAS Studio tasks. You learned how to select data files from the SASHELP library, move, sort, and resize columns, and how to filter rows of a table. The next step is to perform these operations on your own data. Chapter 3 shows you how to import data from Excel workbooks or raw data form text files and create SAS data sets.

Chapter 3: Importing Data into SAS

Introduction

Now that you have learned how to perform some simple tasks using one of the built-in SASHELP data sets, it's time to see how to import your own data into a SAS library. SAS data sets contain two parts: one is called the data descriptor, also known as metadata. Metadata is a fancy word for data about your data. In the case of a SAS data set, this portion of the data set contains such information as the number of rows and columns in the table, the column names, the data type for each column (SAS has only two data types—character and numeric), and other information about how the data set was created.

The second part of a SAS data set contains the actual data values. If you tried to examine a SAS data set using another program such as Word or Notebook, it would show up as nonsense. Only SAS can read, write, and analyze data in a SAS data set. If you have data in Excel workbooks or text files, you need to convert that data into a SAS data set before you can use SAS to modify or analyze the data.

In this chapter, you will see how easy it is to import your own data from Excel workbooks, CSV files, and many other file formats such as Microsoft Access and SPSS, and create SAS data sets.

Exploring the Utilities Tab

Start by clicking the Tasks and Utilities tab in the navigation pane. It looks like this:

Figure 1: The Tasks and Utilities Tab in the Navigation Pane

When you click this tab, you see two separate tabs, one labeled Tasks, the other labeled Utilities. Expanding the Utilities tab displays three sub-tabs: Import Data, Query, and SAS Program (see Figure 2 below):

Figure 2: Expanding the Utilities Tab

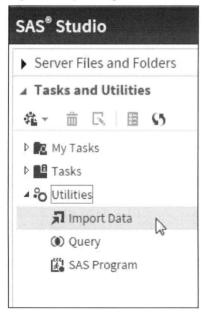

The Import Data task is used to import data in a variety of formats and to create SAS data sets. A complete list of supported file types is shown in Figure 3 below:

Figure 3: List of Supported Files

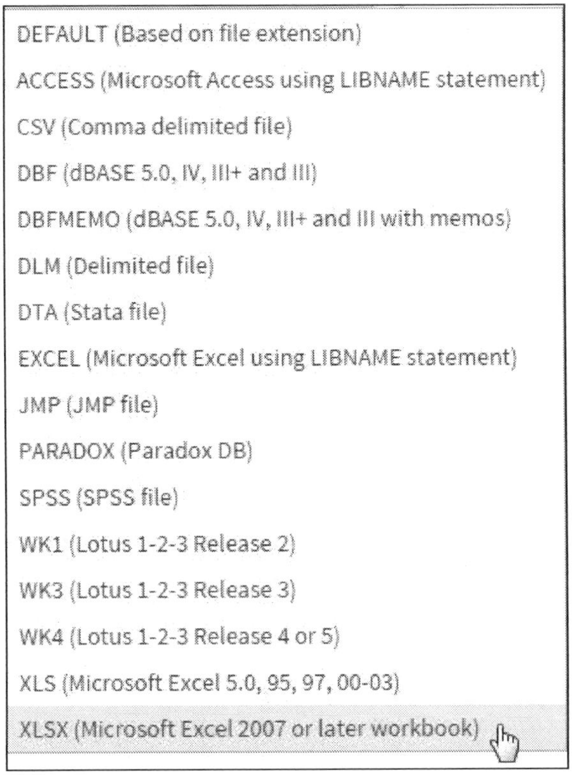

DEFAULT (Based on file extension)

ACCESS (Microsoft Access using LIBNAME statement)

CSV (Comma delimited file)

DBF (dBASE 5.0, IV, III+ and III)

DBFMEMO (dBASE 5.0, IV, III+ and III with memos)

DLM (Delimited file)

DTA (Stata file)

EXCEL (Microsoft Excel using LIBNAME statement)

JMP (JMP file)

PARADOX (Paradox DB)

SPSS (SPSS file)

WK1 (Lotus 1-2-3 Release 2)

WK3 (Lotus 1-2-3 Release 3)

WK4 (Lotus 1-2-3 Release 4 or 5)

XLS (Microsoft Excel 5.0, 95, 97, 00-03)

XLSX (Microsoft Excel 2007 or later workbook)

As you can see, this import data utility can import data from many of the most common PC data formats. Because Excel workbooks and CSV files are so popular, let's use them to demonstrate how SAS converts various file formats into SAS data sets.

The Excel selection can accept both the older XLS workbooks as well as the current form with XLSX extensions. The import data task can use file extensions to automatically determine the file type. If you have a nonstandard file extension or if you prefer to manually select a file format, you can use the dropdown list in Figure 3 to instruct SAS how to convert your file.

Importing Data from an Excel Workbook

Your virtual machine is running a Linux operating system where naming conventions for files are different from the naming conventions used on Microsoft or Apple computers. Filenames in Linux are case sensitive, and folders and subfolders are separated by forward slashes. Filenames on Microsoft platforms are not case sensitive, and folders and subfolders are separated by backward slashes. To help resolve these file-naming conventions, you set up shared folders in your virtual machine that allow your SAS programs to read and write files to the hard drive on your computer.

There are slight differences in how you create shared folders, depending on whether you are running VirtualBox, VMware Workstation Player, or VMware Fusion. The easiest way to read and write data between your SAS Studio session and your hard drive is to place your data files in a specific location—\SASUniversityEdition\myfolders. If you followed the installation directions for your choice of virtualization software, this location on your hard drive is mapped to a shared folder called /folders/myfolders in SAS Studio.

For most of the examples in this book, the location c:\SASUniversityEdition\myfolders is the folder where your data files and SAS data sets are located. All the programs and data files that you place in \SASUniversityEdition\myfolders will show up when you click the My Folders tab in the Navigation pane. Later on, you will see how to set up other shared folders that allow you to read files from any location on your computer.

Let's use the workbook Grades.xlsx (located in the folder c:\SASUniversityEdition\myfolders) for this demonstration.

Note: This file is one of many files stored in a ZIP file containing all the sample data and programs referred to in this book. You can download it from support.sas.com/cody and unzip it into the c:\SASUniversityEdition\myfolders folder.

If you open this workbook in Excel, it looks like this:

Figure 4: Excel Workbook Grades.xlsx

	A	B	C	D	E	F	G	H
1	Name	ID	Quiz1	Quiz2	Midterm	Quiz3	Quiz4	Final
2	Jones	12345	88	80	76	88	90	82
3	Hildebran	22222	95	92	91	94	90	96
4	O'Brien	33333	76	78	79	81	83	80
5								

The first row of the worksheet contains column names (also known as variable names). The remaining rows contain data on three students (yup, it was a very small class). The worksheet name was not changed so that it has the default name Sheet1.

The first step to import this data into a SAS data set is to double-click the Import Data task.

Figure 5: Double-Clicking the Import Data Task

You have two ways to select which file you want to import. One is to click the Select File button on the right side of the screen—the other method is to click the Server Files and Folders tab in the Navigation pane (on the left), find the file, and drag it to the Drag and Drop area.

Clicking Select File brings up a window where you can select a file to import. Here it is:

Figure 6: Clicking on the Select File Button

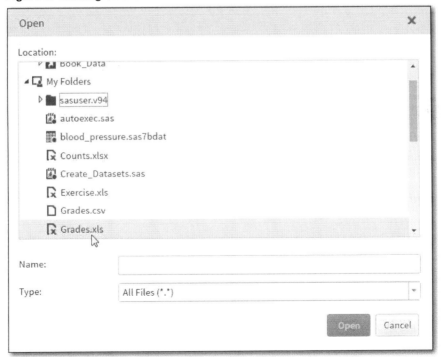

Select the file that you want to import and click Open. This brings up the Import Window:

Figure 7: The Import Window

Use the mouse to enlarge the top half of the Import window or use the scroll bar on the right to reveal the entire window. The figure below shows the expanded view of the Import window:

Figure 8: Expanded View of the Import Window

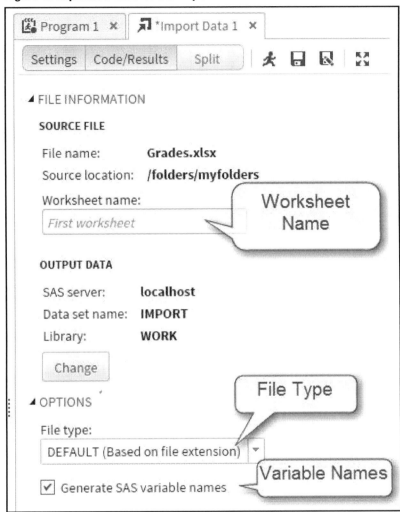

The top part of the window shows information on the file that you want to import. You can enter a Worksheet Name (if there are multiple worksheets). But because you only have one worksheet, you do not have to enter a worksheet name.

The OPTIONS pulldown menu allows you to select a file type. However, if your file has the appropriate extension (for example, XLSX, XLS, or CSV), you can leave the default actions (based on the file extension) to decide how to import the data.

Because the first row of the spreadsheet contains column names, leave the check on the "Generate SAS variable names" option. This tells the import utility to use the first row of the worksheet to generate variable names.

You probably want to change the name of the output SAS data set. Clicking the CHANGE button in the Output Data area of the screen brings up a list of SAS libraries (below):

Figure 9: Changing the Name of the SAS Data Set

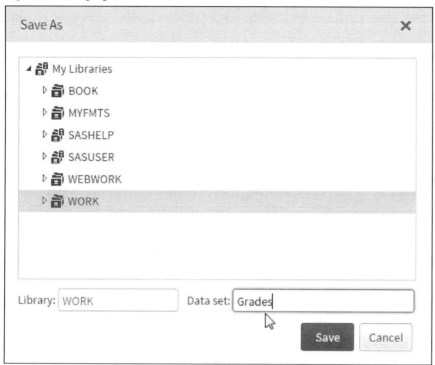

The WORK library is used to create a temporary SAS data set (that disappears when you close your SAS Session). For now, let's select the WORK library and name the data set Grades.

When all is ready, click the RUN icon (Figure 10 below).

Figure 10: Click the Run Icon

You are done! Here is a section of the results:

Figure 11: Variable List for the Work.Grades SAS Data Set

			Alphabetic List of Variables and Attributes			
#	Variable	Type	Len	Format	Informat	Label
8	Final	Num	8	BEST.		Final
2	ID	Num	8	BEST.		ID
5	Midterm	Num	8	BEST.		Midterm
1	Name	Char	10	$10.	$10.	Name
3	Quiz1	Num	8	BEST.		Quiz1
4	Quiz2	Num	8	BEST.		Quiz2
6	Quiz3	Num	8	BEST.		Quiz3
7	Quiz4	Num	8	BEST.		Quiz4

Here you see a list of the variable names, whether they are stored as numeric or character, along with some other information that we don't need at this time. Notice that the import utility correctly read Name as character and the other variables as numeric.

Listing the SAS Data Set

A quick way to see a listing of the Grades data set is to select the LIBRARIES tab in the navigation pane, open the Work library, and double-click Grades. It looks like this:

Figure 12: Data Set Grades in the Work Library

Total rows: 3   Total columns: 8   Rows 1-3

	Name	ID	Quiz1	Quiz2
1	Jones	12345	88	80
2	Hildebrand	22222	95	92
3	O'Brien	33333	76	78

You can use your mouse to scroll to the right to see the rest of the table. To create a nicer looking report, click the Tasks and Utilities tab of the navigation pane and select Data followed by List data, like this:

Figure 13: The List Data Task

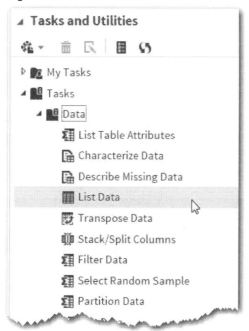

Double-click List Data, and select the Grades data set in the WORK library. Then click the RUN icon. You will be presented with a nice looking list of the Grades data set (see Figure 14 below):

Figure 14: List of the Grades Data Set

List Data for WORK.GRADES

Obs	Name	ID	Quiz1	Quiz2	Midterm	Quiz3	Quiz4	Final
1	Jones	12345	88	80	76	88	90	82
2	Hildebrand	22222	95	92	91	94	90	96
3	O'Brien	33333	76	78	79	81	83	80

Importing an Excel Workbook with Invalid SAS Variable Names

What if your Excel worksheet has column headings that are not valid SAS variable names?

> Valid SAS variable names are up to 32 characters long. The first character must be a letter or underscore—the remaining characters can be letters, digits, or underscores. You are free to use upper- or lowercase letters.

As an example of a worksheet with invalid variable names, take a look at the worksheet Grades2 shown in Figure 15:

Figure 15: List of Excel Workbook Grades2

	A	B	C	D	E	F	G	H
1	Stuent Name	ID	Quiz 1	Quiz 2	Mid Term	Quiz 3	Quiz 4	2015Final
2	Jones	12345	88	80	76	88	90	82
3	Hildebrand	22222	95	92	91	94	90	96
4	O'Brien	33333	76	78	79	81	83	80
5								

Most of the column headings in this spreadsheet are not valid SAS variable names. Six of them contain a blank, and the last column (2015Final) starts with a digit. What happens when you import this worksheet? Because you now know how to use the Import Data task, it is not necessary to describe the import task again. All you really need to see is the final list of variables in the data set. Here they are:

Figure 16: Variable Names in the Grades2 SAS Data Set

	Alphabetic List of Variables and Attributes					
#	Variable	Type	Len	Format	Informat	Label
2	ID	Num	8	BEST.		ID
5	Mid_Term	Num	8	BEST.		Mid Term
3	Quiz_1	Num	8	BEST.		Quiz 1
4	Quiz_2	Num	8	BEST.		Quiz 2
6	Quiz_3	Num	8	BEST.		Quiz 3
7	Quiz_4	Num	8	BEST.		Quiz 4
1	Stuent_Name	Char	10	$10.	$10.	Stuent Name
8	_2015Final	Num	8	BEST.		2015Final

As you can see, SAS replaced all the blanks with underscores and added an underscore as the first character in the 2015Final name to create valid SAS variable names.

Importing an Excel Workbook That Does Not Have Column Headings

What if the first row of your worksheet does not contain column headings (variable names)? You have two choices: First, you can edit the worksheet and insert a row with column headings. The other option is to uncheck "Create Variable Names" in the options section in the Import Window (see Figure 17) and let SAS create variable names for you.

Figure 17: Uncheck the Create Variable Names Option

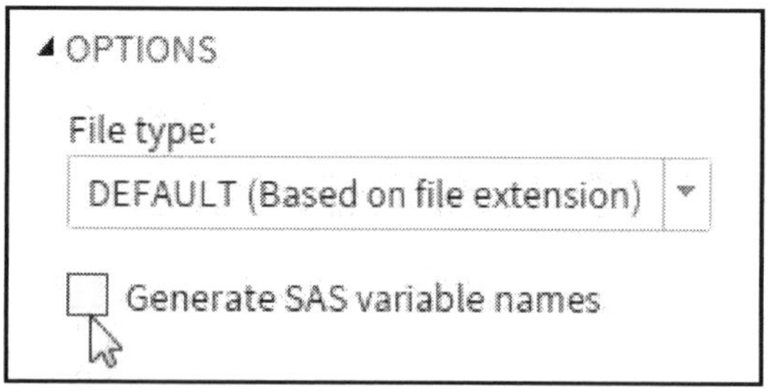

Here is the result:

Figure 18: Variable Names Generated by SAS

#	Variable	Type	Len	Format	Informat	Label
1	A	Num	8	BEST.		A
2	B	Char	1	$1.	$1.	B
3	C	Num	8	MMDDYY10.		C
4	D	Num	8	BEST.		D
5	E	Num	8	BEST.		E
6	F	Char	1	$1.	$1.	F

Alphabetic List of Variables and Attributes

SAS used the column identifiers (A through F) as variable names. You can leave these variable names as they are or change them using DATA step programming. Another option is to use PROC DATASETS, a SAS procedure that allows you to alter various attributes of a SAS data set without having to create a new copy of the data set.

When you import a CSV file without variable names, you will see variable names VAR1, VAR2, etc., that are generated by SAS.

Importing Data from a CSV File

CSV (comma-separated values) files are a popular format for external data files. As the name implies, CSV files use commas as data delimiters. Many web sites allow you to download data as CSV files. As with Excel workbooks, your CSV file may or may not contain variable names at the beginning of the file. If the file does contain variable names, make sure that the "Generate SAS Variable Names" options box is checked; if not, uncheck this option.

As an example, take a look at the CSV file called Grades.csv in Figure 19 below:

Figure 19: CSV File Grades.csv

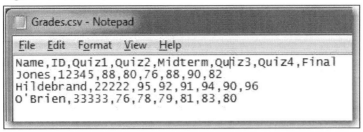

This CSV file contains the same data as the Excel Workbook Grades.xlsx. Notice that variable names are included in the file. You can import this file and create a SAS data set, using the same steps that you used to import the Excel workbook. The import facility will automatically use the correct code to import this data file because of the CSV file extension. The resulting SAS data set is identical to the one shown in Figure 14.

Shared Folders (Accessing Data from Anywhere on Your Hard Drive)

When you follow the instructions in setting up SAS Studio, a default folder referred to in SAS Studio as /folders/myfolders allows you to read data from the folder called \SASUniversityEdition\myfolders on your hard drive. If this is the only place where you plan to read data, you can skip the remainder of this section. However, if you need to read data from other folders on your hard drive, you will need to learn how to create shared folders. This may seem a bit scary, but if you repeat the steps in the example that follows, you should be successful.

For this example, a folder called **c:\Books\Book_Data** was created on the hard drive.

To create a shared folder, click Settings before starting your virtual machine.

Note: Your virtual machine should be either off or running, not in a suspended state. We recommend that you abort (turn off) your virtual machine when you are creating (or removing) folders.

Figure 20: Click the Settings Icon

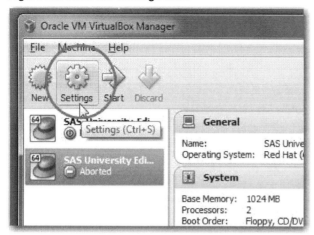

Under the Settings menu, select **Shared Folders**.

Figure 21: Select Shared Folders

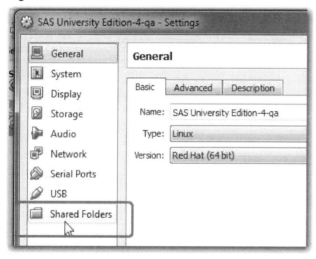

To add a new folder, click the plus (+) sign as shown in Figure 22:

Figure 22: Click the + Sign to Add a Folder

In the Folder Path pull-down list, select **Other.**

Figure 23: In the Pull-Down List, Choose Other

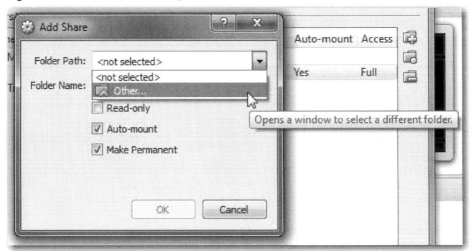

Browse the list to locate the folder **c:\Books\Book_Data**.

If you type in a folder name instead of browsing for it, be sure to use the same case (upper-mixed case or lowercase) for the folder name.

Figure 24: Browse and Select Your Folder

Make sure that the two boxes labeled "Auto-mount" and "Make Permanent" are checked. Note: Depending on how you choose your folder, the selection "Make Permanent" may not be listed. This is OK.

Figure 25: Check Auto-Mount and Make Permanent

Click OK and the folder name is automatically created.

Note: The folder name cannot contain any blanks. If the folder name on your hard drive contains blanks, either leave them out in the Folder Name being created or replace them with underscores.

Your new folder should now show up in the list of folders on your virtual machine.

Figure 26: Your Folder Is Created

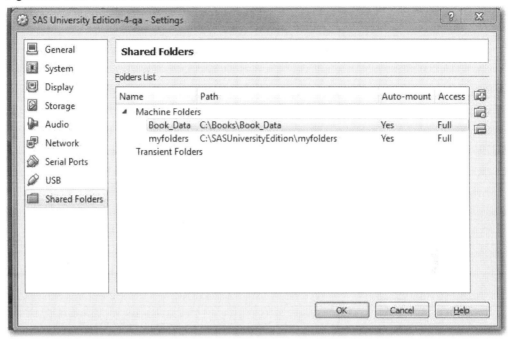

If your virtual machine was off, restart it. (You can do this by clicking Machine and selecting the Start option. You can also double-click the virtual machine that you wish to restart in the list of virtual machines (you may only have one in the list).

Figure 27: Restart Your Virtual Machine

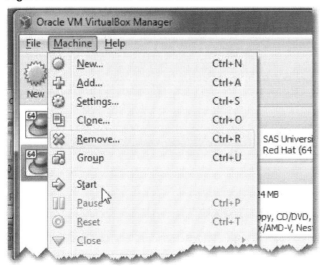

When you open SAS Studio, you will see your new folder under the heading of Folder Shortcuts. (If your Studio session was already open, you need to restart it).

Figure 28: Your New Folder in Studio

Demonstrating How to Read Data from a Shared Folder

The last section in this chapter demonstrates how to read data from a shared folder. An Excel file called Demographics.xlsx contains some demographic data on four subjects and was placed on the hard drive in c:\Books\Book_Data. It is listed in Figure 29 (below):

Figure 29: File Demographic.xlsx in C:\Books\Book_Data

	A	B	C	D
1	Subj	Gender	Height	Weight
2	1	M	68	150
3	2	F	62	110
4	3	F	64	135
5	4	M	70	210
6				

To read this workbook and convert it into a SAS data set, follow the same steps as in the previous demonstration of reading a workbook from the \SASUniversityEdition\myfolders location. But when you browse for a file, select Demographics.xlsx in the Book_Data Folder Shortcut (Figure 30 below):

Figure 30: Select Demographics.xlsx from the Book_Data Folder Shortcut

Conclusions

In this chapter, you saw how to import data from Excel workbooks and CSV files. Importing data from any of the other choices displayed in Figure 3 is basically the same as importing data from Excel workbooks and CSV files. If your data resides in text files (either in fixed columns or separated by delimiters), read the next chapter to learn how to create SAS data sets from these types of files. Finally, you saw how to create a shared folder and read data from locations on your hard drive other than \SASUniversityEdition\myfolders.

Problems

3-1: Use the Import Utility to create a temporary SAS data set called Clinical using the Excel workbook ClinicData.xlsx. Use the List Data task to list the data set.

3-2: Use the Import Utility to create a temporary SAS data set called Diabetes, using the Excel workbook Diabetes.xls. Use the List Data task to list the first five rows of the table.

3-3: Repeat problem 3-2 except use the CSV file Diabetes.csv as the source of your data.

3-4: Using the SAS data set Diabetes, use a filter to display all subjects with blood glucose levels (variable Glucose) above 400. You can do this by using the temporary SAS data set you created in Problems 2 or 3, or you can try to use the permanent SAS data set Diabetes that you downloaded to your hard drive. Refer to the Problem Instructions section of this book if you forgot how to create a libref.

Chapter 4: Reading Data from Text Files

Introduction

You may have data in text files, either separated by delimiters or arranged in columns. In order to import data of this type, you will need to write a SAS program. Don't panic. It's not that hard to do, and at some point in your education, you may need to go beyond what the SAS Studio point-and-click environment can do for you.

If your data is in one of the formats described in the last chapter (Excel, CSV, Access, SPSS, etc.), you can skip this chapter. However, this chapter also covers some basics of SAS programming that will be useful if you need to do more advanced data manipulation or if you work in a company or university where SAS Studio is not available and you have to write your own programs. For a more detailed discussion of SAS programming, please take a look at *Learning SAS by Example* (Cody, 2007) or *Introduction to SAS University Edition* (Cody, 2015), both available from SAS Press (**support.sas.com/cody**).

Understanding the Work Area

So far in this book, you have been exploring the Navigation pane on the left side of the SAS Studio screen. It's now time to shift your attention to the work area on the right side of the screen. Below is an expanded view of the work area (Figure 1 below):

Figure 1: Expanded View of the Work Area

There are three tabs: CODE, LOG, and RESULTS. The CODE tab is where you write your SAS programs. After you run a program, the LOG tab displays your program, any syntax errors that you made, information about data being read or written, and some information about CPU time and other resources that were used. Finally, the RESULT tab is where the output (tables, statistical tables, graphs, etc.) appear.

SAS programs consist of two main sections: DATA steps, where you read, write, and process data, and PROC (short for procedure) steps where you provide information to built-in procedures that create reports, graphs, or perform statistical tests. DATA steps begin with the keyword DATA and usually end with a RUN statement; PROC steps begin with the keyword PROC and usually end with a RUN or QUIT statement.

Some Basic Rules of SAS Programs

As with all programming languages, SAS has syntax and logic rules that must be followed. The first rule is that every SAS statement ends with a semicolon.

This is a good place to mention that one of the most common programming mistakes, especially with beginning SAS programmers, is to forget a semicolon at the end of a statement. This sometimes leads to confusing error messages.

When you write a program, you can place several statements on a single line if you end each statement with a semicolon. (Note: This practice is not recommended—it makes programs hard to read.) Next, a SAS statement can use as many lines as necessary. Many SAS programmers leave blank lines between sections of their programs to make the program easier to read.

Next, there are some naming conventions for data set names, SAS column (variable) names, and other entities that you will encounter later. Most SAS names comply with the following rule:

> SAS names are a maximum of 32 characters in length. They must begin with a letter or underscore (_). The remaining characters in a SAS name are letters, numbers, or underscores. Spaces are not allowed in any SAS name.

If you are introducing a new column name in a program, you are free to use uppercase, lowercase, or mixed case. SAS names are not case-sensitive. However, SAS remembers the case that you used the first time the column or variable name is written and will use that case in all of the reports and listings produced by the program, even if you write the column name differently elsewhere in the program.

Here are some examples of valid and invalid SAS names:

Valid SAS Names
My_Data
HeightWeight
X123
_123
Price_per_pound

Invalid SAS Names	
My Data	Contains an invalid character (space)
123xyz	Starts with a digit
Temperature-Data	Contains an invalid character (-)
Group%	Contains an invalid character (%)

Writing a Program to Read a Text File Where Data Values Are Separated by Delimiters

In the last chapter, you saw how to read CSV (comma-separated values) files using the Import task under the Utilities tab. When the first row of the file contains column names, SAS can use those names when creating the SAS data set. When the first row of the file does not contain column names, SAS names the columns Var1, Var2, Var3, and so forth.

There are two reasons to write a SAS program to read delimited data: First, if your CSV file does not have column names in the first row and you do not want SAS to name your columns Var1, Var2, Var3, etc., you can write a short program to read the file and assign your own column names. Second, you may have a file with other delimiters such as spaces or pipes (the | symbol) instead of commas.

To demonstrate this process, a file called Health_List.txt was created in a folder called c:\SASUniversityEdition\myfolders (the shared folder that is created if you follow the installation instructions for SAS University Edition). The file uses spaces as delimiters and contains some demographic and health data. A description of the file is shown in Figure 2:

Figure 2: Description of the Blank Delimited File Helth_List.txt

Variable Name	Description
Subj	Subject number
Gender	Gender (M or F)
Age	Age in years
HR	Heart rate
SBP	Systolic blood pressure
DBP	Diastolic blood pressure
Chol	Total cholesterol

A listing of the file is shown in Figure 3:

Figure 3: File Health_List.txt (located in c:\SASUniversityEdition\myfolders)

```
001 M 23 68 120 90 128
002  F 55  72    180 90 170
003 F 18 58 118 72 122
004 M  80 82 . . 220
005 F 34 62 128 80 .
006   F  38 78 108 68 220
```

There are several important features of this text file. First, one or more successive spaces represent a single delimiter. Next, a period was used to represent a missing value. These two properties of this text files are what SAS uses as defaults in a type of input called List Input.

You can write a very short program to read this text file and create a SAS dataset. Here is the beginning of such a program, written under the CODE tab in SAS Studio (Figure 4):

Figure 4: Starting to Write a Program to Read the Text File Helth_List.txt and Create a SAS Data Set

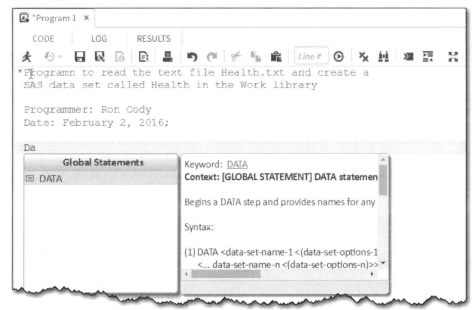

The first six lines of this program constitute a comment statement. If you have written programs in other computer languages, you are, no doubt, familiar with comment statements. Comment statements are ignored by the computer (they are not compiled or interpreted) but are very useful for you or someone else trying to understand what the program does, who wrote it, and when.

> SAS COMMENT statements begin with an asterisk (*) and end with a semicolon. Following the rules about SAS statements mentioned earlier, the COMMENT statement above uses several lines and even contains a blank line.

Following the comment, you see the first two letters of the word data. DATA is the keyword that begins a DATA step, the place where you read and write data and perform computations and/or logical actions. As you begin to type the word "data", the SAS Studio editor causes a syntax box to appear, giving you information about the syntax of the statement that you are starting to type.

Once you are familiar with SAS programming, you may want to turn off the Auto-Complete feature of SAS Studio. Here's how to do this (along with setting a few additional editor options):

First click the Menu icon (Figure 5):

Figure 5: The Menu Icon

This brings up the following screen:

Figure 6: The Preferences Menu

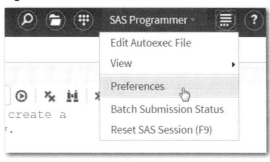

Click Editor in the list of options:

Figure 7: List of Editor Preferences

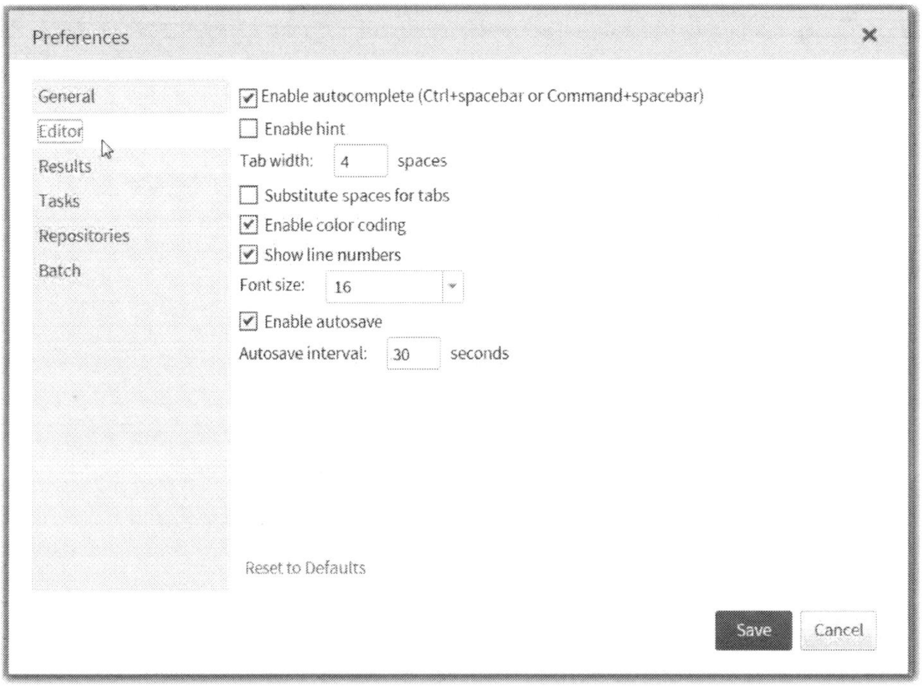

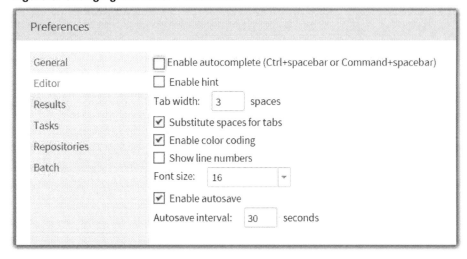

You can select or deselect any of these options, as well as choose the number of spaces to indent when you press the Tab key; the font size; and an option concerning the Autosave feature. The next figure shows this author's preferences:

Figure 8: Changing the Editor Preferences

You see that autocomplete and Enable hint are turned off; the tab width is set to 3 (this author's usual choice); the option to substitute spaces for tabs is selected; and the Font size is set to 16. Once you are finished with the Editor options, click the SAVE box at the bottom of the screen.

Now, back to the program. Figure 9 shows a listing of the completed program:

Figure 9: Completed Program

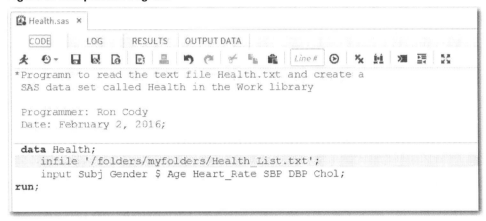

```
* Programn to read the text file Health.txt and create a
  SAS data set called Health in the Work library

  Programmer: Ron Cody
  Date: February 2, 2016;

data Health;
   infile '/folders/myfolders/Health_List.txt';
   input Subj Gender $ Age Heart_Rate SBP DBP Chol;
run;
```

You have already seen the COMMENT statement. The DATA statement lets you choose a name for the SAS data set that you want to create (Health in this example). The INFILE statement tells the program where to find the text file Health_List.txt. Remember that the actual location for this file was c:\SASUniversityEdition\myfolders. This is a shared folder and you refer to it in your program as /folders/myfolders/Health_List.txt. The shared folder name is placed in either single or double quotation marks.

Finally, the INPUT statement lists the names of each of the columns in the data set that you are creating. This type of INPUT statement (there are other types) is called 'list input'. Unless you indicate otherwise, SAS treats multiple delimiters (such as multiple blanks or commas in a row) as a single delimiter.

Because Gender is a character value, you indicate this to SAS by following the column name with a dollar sign ($). You end the DATA step with a RUN statement.

> By default, placing a dollar sign in an INPUT statement when you are reading delimited data, allows you to read up to eight characters.

You will see shortly how to change the default length to a length appropriate for your character values. It's time to run your program. Click the Run icon.

Figure 10: Click the Run Icon

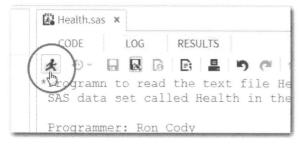

You should see the following:

Figure 11: The RESULTS Window

Here you see all the columns selected and a display of the data. (Before this screen shot was taken, the author right-clicked on the top line (where you see the column names) and the option "Size grid columns to contents" was selected.)

Before you celebrate, you should (always) check the SAS log. Click the LOG tab to do this. It looks like this:

Figure 12: Inspecting the Log

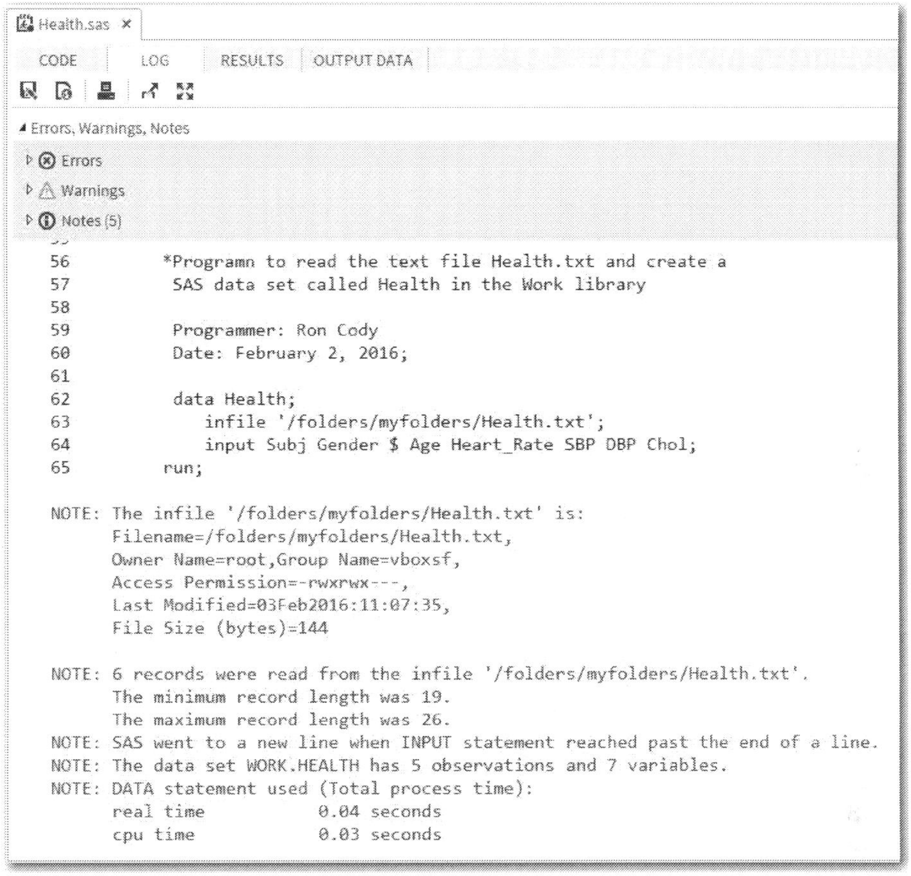

```
 Health.sas  ×

  CODE        LOG        RESULTS    OUTPUT DATA

  ▲ Errors, Warnings, Notes

  ▷ ⊗ Errors

  ▷ ⚠ Warnings

  ▷ ⓘ Notes (5)

    56          *Programn to read the text file Health.txt and create a
    57           SAS data set called Health in the Work library
    58
    59           Programmer: Ron Cody
    60           Date: February 2, 2016;
    61
    62           data Health;
    63               infile '/folders/myfolders/Health.txt';
    64               input Subj Gender $ Age Heart_Rate SBP DBP Chol;
    65           run;

 NOTE: The infile '/folders/myfolders/Health.txt' is:
       Filename=/folders/myfolders/Health.txt,
       Owner Name=root,Group Name=vboxsf,
       Access Permission=-rwxrwx---,
       Last Modified=03Feb2016:11:07:35,
       File Size (bytes)=144

 NOTE: 6 records were read from the infile '/folders/myfolders/Health.txt'.
       The minimum record length was 19.
       The maximum record length was 26.
 NOTE: SAS went to a new line when INPUT statement reached past the end of a line.
 NOTE: The data set WORK.HEALTH has 5 observations and 7 variables.
 NOTE: DATA statement used (Total process time):
       real time           0.04 seconds
       cpu time            0.03 seconds
```

The very top of the log show Errors, Warnings, and Notes. If you have any errors or warnings, you can scroll down to view them. As an alternative, you double-click the errors or warnings heading to display a list of all the errors or warnings. You will see a demonstration of this later in this chapter.

Because your program ran successfully, it's time to save it. Click the File Save icon, select the folder where you want the program to be stored, name the file, and click Save (Figure 13):

Figure 13: Saving and Naming Your Program

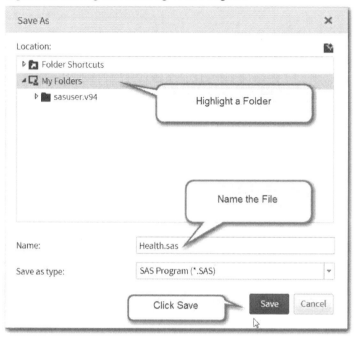

Viewing Errors and Warnings

To demonstrate how the Errors and Warnings indicators work, an error was introduced in the program (the data set name was changed to 123Health, an invalid name). Here is the log from the modified program:

Figure 14: Log Showing an Error

```
⊗ Health.sas  ×

  CODE        LOG        RESULTS
  ⊠ ⬜ ⬛ ⬆ ⤯ ⤢

◢ Errors, Warnings, Notes
▷ ⊗ Errors (2)
▷ ⚠ Warnings (2)
▷ ⓘ Notes (2)
    61
    62            data 123Health;
                         ⎯⎯⎯
                         22
                         200
    ERROR 22-322: Syntax error, expecting one of the following: a name, a quoted string, /, ;, _DATA_, _LAST_, _NULL_.

    ERROR 200-322: The symbol is not recognized and will be ignored.

    63            infile '/folders/m
```

Because this program has so few lines, the error shows up without your having to scroll down. However, when you write longer programs, you can see each of the errors by placing the cursor on the Errors heading (as shown in Figure 14) and double-clicking. This brings up a list of errors like this:

Figure 15: Double-click the Errors Heading

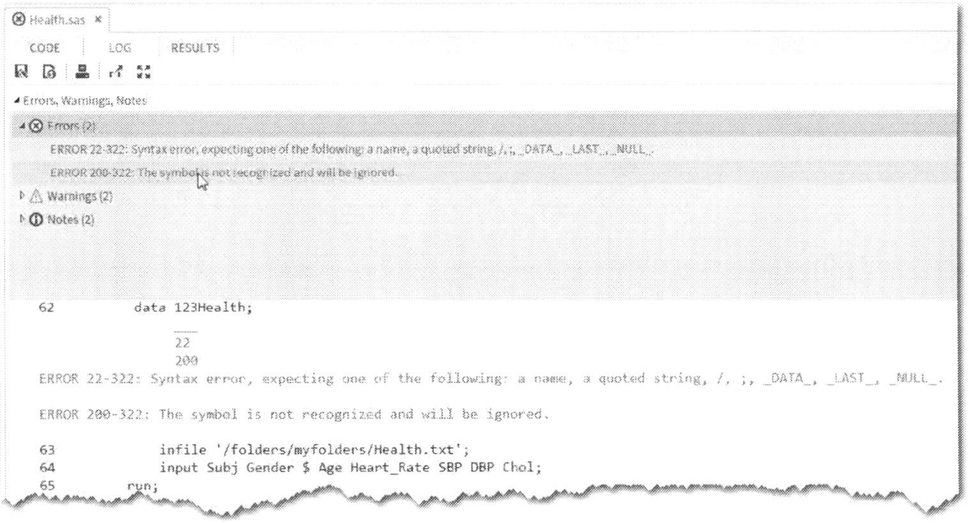

You can click on any of the errors to jump to the portion of the program where the error occurred.

> One hint about error messages: One single error can often result in several error messages, making them difficult to interpret. If you fix one error, it is possible that other error messages disappear when you run the program again.

Reading CSV Files

Commas are one of the most popular delimiters. In the previous chapter, you saw how to use the Import Data task to read CSV files. CSV files use commas as delimiters; and if there are two commas together, it is assumed that there is a missing value for that column.

The same data contained in the Health_List.txt file was converted to a CSV file called Health.csv and is listed below:

Figure 16: Listing of File Health.csv

```
001,M,23,68,120,90,128
002,F,55,72,180,90,170
003,F,18,58,118,72,122
004,M,80,82,,,220
005,F,34,62,128,80,,
006,F,38,78,108,68,220
```

Because this is a CSV file where two commas together represent a missing value, there is no need to use a period to represent a missing value as was the case with the space-delimited file.

You could read this file using the Import Utility, but the column names would be Var1, Var2, etc. (You would also have to uncheck the option to generate SAS names when using the utility.) You can write a short SAS program, similar to the program you used to read the Health_List.txt file. The only change you need to make is to add the DSD (Delimiter-Sensitive Data) option in the INFILE statement. You place INFILE options after you specify the file location. The DSD option performs several actions: One is to use commas as delimiters; the other is to interpret two successive commas to mean that there is a missing value for the next value being read. Here is a program that can read the Health.csv file:

Figure 17: Program to Read the Health.csv File

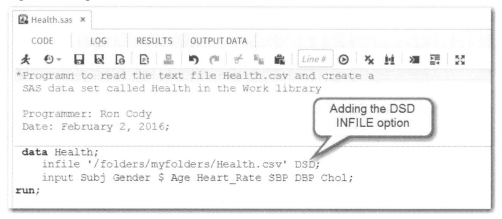

The resulting data set is identical to the one previously created from the Health_List.txt file.

Reading Text Files with Other Delimiters

You may encounter files with delimiters other than blanks or commas. These files may follow the rule that you treat multiple delimiters as a single delimiter (as with the program in Figure 9), or they may follow the rule that multiple delimiters represent missing values (as with CSV files).

You can address both of these issues easily. First, you can add an INFILE option called DLM= to specify one or more delimiter characters (even non-printing ones such as tabs) that were used in the file. Next, if your delimiters are treated similar to the way commas are treated in CSV files, add the option DSD as well.

Here are several examples of INFILE statements to demonstrate how to use these two options:

- You have a comma-delimited file, but you want multiple commas to be treated as a single delimiter:

```
INFILE '/folders/myfolders/your_file' DLM=',';
```

- You have a file where tabs are the delimiters, and you want multiple tabs to be treated as a single delimiter:

  ```
  INFILE '/folders/myfolders/your_file' DLM='09'x;
  ```

  Because tabs are non-printing characters, you refer to them using what is called a hexadecimal constant. In ASCII, a tab is coded as 09. You represent this value in a SAS DATA step by placing the '09' in single or double quotation marks and following it with an upper- or lowercase x.

- You have a file where commas, question marks, and dollar signs are delimiters, and you want to treat any two delimiters together to indicate a missing value (as with CSV files):

  ```
  INFILE '/folders/myfolders/your_file' DLM=',?$' DSD;
  ```

  In this example, you use both the DLM= and DSD options. DLM= lets you supply the list of possible delimiters, and the DSD option treats multiple delimiters together to indicate that there are multiple missing values. Remember, without the DLM= option, using DSD assumes the default delimiter is a comma (it was created specifically to read CSV files).

Setting the Length of Character Variables

In the previous program, you placed a dollar sign after the column Gender to tell the program that Gender was a character variable. Although the program runs OK, the storage length for Gender is eight bytes (characters) because that is the default length for list input when a length is not defined. In most cases, you want to specify an appropriate length for every character variable in your data set. Why? Two reasons: If your variable is shorter than eight (Gender is only a single character), you are wasting storage space. If your character variable is longer than eight characters, it will be truncated.

One way to specify the length of each character column (variable) is to add a LENGTH statement before the INPUT statement. The syntax for the LENGTH statement is:

```
LENGTH Column-Name(s) $ n Column-Name(s) $ n;
```

where `Column-Names(s)` is a single column name or a list of column names (if they are all going to have the same length). The 'n' in the `$n` part of the statement is the length assigned to the preceding column name(s). For example, to assign a length of one to Gender, the LENGTH statement would read:

```
Length Gender $ 1;
```

It is important that the LENGTH statement come before the INPUT statement. Here's the reason: SAS determines the length of all columns by first scanning the program, looking for column names. The first time it sees a column name, it assigns a length, based on how the column is referenced. If you do not use a LENGTH statement as in Figure 17, SAS uses a default length of eight. If you placed the LENGTH statement after the INPUT statement, the length would already have been set to eight and the LENGTH statement would be ignored.

As a further example, the following LENGTH statement sets a length of one for the columns Ques1-Ques10, a length of 15 for column Last_Name, and a length of 11 for the column SS:

```
LENGTH Ques1-Ques10 $ 1 Last_Name $ 15 SS $ 11;
```

By the way, as you probably guessed, the notation Ques1-Ques10 refers to 10 columns Ques1, Ques2, up to Ques10.

If you want to modify the program displayed in Figure 17 to define a length of one for Gender, the entire program would look like this:

Figure 18: Adding a LENGTH Statement

Reading Text Data in Fixed Columns

The last section of this chapter shows you how to read text data where the data values are placed in predefined columns. A data definition for a file that contains the same information as the Health_list.txt and Health.csv files is listed below:

Columns in the Health Data File

Variable Name	Description	Starting Column	Number of Columns
Subj	Subject number	1	3
Gender	Gender (M or F)	4	1
Age	Age in years	5	2
Heart_Rate	Heart rate	7	2
SBP	Systolic blood pressure	9	3

Variable Name	Description	Starting Column	Number of Columns
DBP	Diastolic blood pressure	12	3
Chol	Total cholesterol	16	3

The data file looks like this:

```
1234567890123456789012345678901234567890 (Ruler - this line is not in the file)
001M2368120 90128
002F5572180 90170
003F1858118 72122
004M8082       220
005F3462128 80
006F3878108 68220
```

With this information, you can now write an INPUT statement. One way of writing such a statement is called "formatted input." It looks like this:

```
Input @1  Subj        3.
      @4  Gender      $1.
      @5  Age         2.
      @7  Heart_Rate  2.
      @9  SBP         3.
      @12 DBP         3.
      @16 Chol        3.;
```

Before each column name, you see an @ sign followed by a number. SAS calls this a column pointer. For example, @7 means "go to column 7." Following the column pointer, you enter a valid column name followed by what SAS calls an INFORMAT. Informats tell the program how to read and interpret the data in the columns following the column pointer. This INPUT statement uses only two informats. The numbers without any dollar signs are numeric informats. They tell the program how many columns of numeric data to read. The numbers (actually only one here) with a dollar sign before them are character informats. They tell the program how many columns of character data to read. Note, that using a character informat in the INPUT statement also defines the storage length for that column.

A complete program to read the file Health.txt is shown next:

Figure 19: Reading Column Data

```
* Programn to read the text file Health.txt and create a
  SAS data set called Health in the Work library

  Programmer: Ron Cody
  Date: February 2, 2016;

data Health;
    infile '/folders/myfolders/Health.txt' pad;
    Input @1  Subj        3.
          @4  Gender      $1.
          @5  Age          2.
          @7  Heart_Rate 2.
          @9  SBP          3.
          @12 DBP          3.
          @16 Chol         3.;
run;
```

Notice one additional option (PAD) that was added to the INFILE statement. The PAD option is needed in case there are some short records in the file. The PAD option says to pad each record with blanks. For example, the line of data for subject 005 is missing a value for cholesterol, and there is a carriage return following the value for diastolic blood pressure (80). If you did not include the PAD option, the program would try to read a value for Chol starting in column 16. This would cause a serious error.

> If you have short records and you do not use the PAD option, SAS will go to the next line to read values. The only way you will know this happened is to read the SAS log and see a note that says that SAS went to a new line.

You can read more about the INPUT statement in *An Introduction to SAS University Edition* (Cody) and *Learning SAS by Example* (Cody), both published by SAS Press.

Conclusions

If you always have data in a standard format such as Excel workbooks, CSV files (with column headings in the first row), or other data types that the Import Utility can read directly, you could have skipped most or all of this chapter. However, there are two good reasons why it was worth your time reading this chapter. First, you now have the tools to read almost any type of raw data file. Second, you now know a little bit about SAS programming and how to use the Code window to write SAS programs.

Even though the Statistics Tasks built into SAS Studio can perform just about any statistical test that you may need, there will be times when you need to manipulate the data or tweak the SAS procedures written by SAS Studio to obtain your result.

Problems

4-1: Write a short DATA step to read the text file Diabetes_No_Varnames.csv and create a temporary SAS data set called Diabetes. The data in this file is the same as the data in the Diabetes.xls file except that the first row does not contain variable (column) names. Use the names Insulin, Subj, Diet_Drinks, and Glucose for the variables. You may decide to make the variable Subj character or numeric, your choice. Use a LENGTH statement to set a length of 1 for the variable Insulin and a length of 9 for Diet_Drinks.

Hint: your INFILE statement should read:

```
Infile '/folders/myfolders/problems/Diabetes_No_Varnames.csv' DSD;
```

4-2: The file Diabetes.txt is a text file with the following layout:

Column Name	Starting Column	Length	Type
Subj	1	2	Character
Insulin	3	1	Character
Diet_Drinks	4	9	Character
Glucose	13	3	Numeric

Write a DATA step to read this text file and create a temporary SAS data set called Diabetes. Hint:

Your INFILE statement should read:

```
infile '/folders/myfolders/problems/Diabetes.txt' pad;
```

4-3: (Advanced) The file Blood_Pressure.txt is a tab-delimited file that contains these variables:

Column Name	Type	Maximum Length
Drug	Character	7
Subj	Numeric	
Gender	Character	1
SBP	Numeric	
DBP	Numeric	

The first row does not contains column names. Also, two tabs together indicate a missing value (hint DSD option).

Here are the first few rows of the file (remember, the delimiter is a tab—not multiple spaces):

```
Placebo      1      F      138      86
Placebo      2      M      124      82
Placebo      3      F      150      72
Placebo      4             136      84
Placebo      5      F
Placebo      6      M      132      84
```

Write a DATA step to read this file and create a temporary SAS data set called Blood_Pressure. Remember that a tab is represented by the Hexidecimal constant '09'x. Make sure that the length for the character variables matches the maximum length in the table above.

Use the List data task to list the first 10 rows of this table.

Chapter 5: Descriptive Statistics – Univariate Analysis

Introduction

Before you begin any statistical test, you should spend some time "getting to know your data." This chapter describes ways to examine both continuous and categorical data using a variety of techniques, including descriptive statistical measures such as means and standard deviations as well as graphical techniques such as histograms and bar charts.

One of the reasons this step is so important is that understanding your data is necessary in choosing appropriate statistical tests to perform. Also, describing your data, especially using graphical techniques, is one way to spot possible errors in your data.

Generating Descriptive Statistics for Continuous Variables

Let's use the SASHELP data set Heart to demonstrate how to produce descriptive statistics for continuous and categorical variables. Start by selecting Summary Statistics from the Statistics tab on the Tasks menu. It looks like this:

Figure 1: Selecting Summary Statistics from the Statistics Task Menu

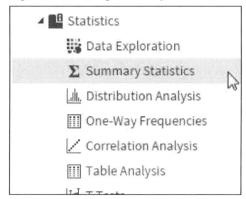

Double-click this selection to bring up the following screen:

Figure 2: DATA Tab for Summary Statistics

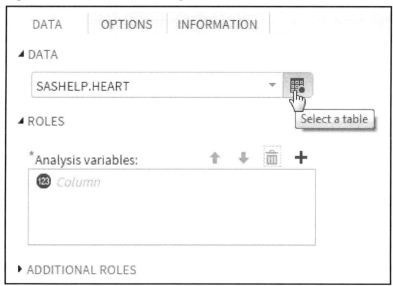

Because you want to analyze data from the Heart data set in the SASHELP library, you click the Select a Table icon, choose the SASHELP library and the Heart data set. This data set contains variables such as Sex, Status (dead or alive), Height, Weight, and several variables related to health risks such as blood pressure, smoking, and cholesterol.

The next step is to select variables to analyze. Click the plus sign to bring up a list of variables in the Heart data set. You can select variables in two ways. One is to hold down the Ctrl key and left-click each of the variables that you want to select. The other method is to click one variable, hold down the Shift key, and then click a variable farther down in the list. All the variables from the first to the last will be selected. You can even combine these two methods to select variables from the list. For this example, you want to select the variables Height, Weight, Diastolic (diastolic blood pressure), and Systolic (systolic blood pressure). Because these variables are all in order in the list, you can use the Shift-key method to select them. It looks like this:

Figure 3: Selecting Variables for Analysis

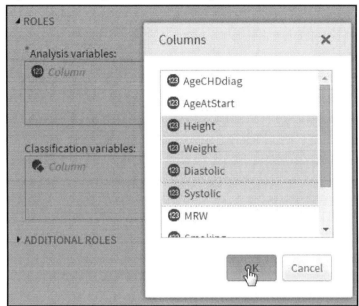

Once you click OK, you can click the OPTIONS tab to select or deselect statistics and plots that you want to generate (Figure 4).

Figure 4: Click the OPTIONS Tab

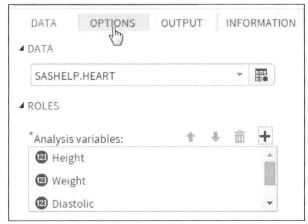

Options for Summary Statistics are as follows:

Figure 5: OPTIONS for Summary Statistics

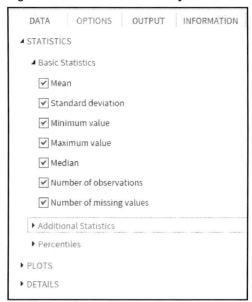

Notice that many of the statistics boxes are already checked. You can select additional statistics or click on a box to deselect a statistic that has already been selected. In this example, the Number of missing values and a request for the median have been added to the default list. It is very useful to see both the number of nonmissing observations along with the number of observations with missing values.

One other useful statistic is the 95% confidence interval (95% CI) for the mean. The 95% confidence interval for the mean is useful to determine how accurately your sample mean estimates the mean of the population from which you drew your sample.

To request this statistic, click the triangle to the left of the heading Additional Statistics. This reveals a further set of choices as shown in Figure 6.

Figure 6: Additional Statistics

> ◢ Additional Statistics
>
> ☐ Standard error
>
> ☐ Variance
>
> ☐ Mode
>
> ☐ Range
>
> ☐ Sum
>
> ☐ Sum of weights
>
> ☑ Confidence limits for the mean
>
>   Confidence level: 95% ▾
>
> ☐ Coefficient of variation
>
> ☐ Skewness
>
> ☐ Kurtosis

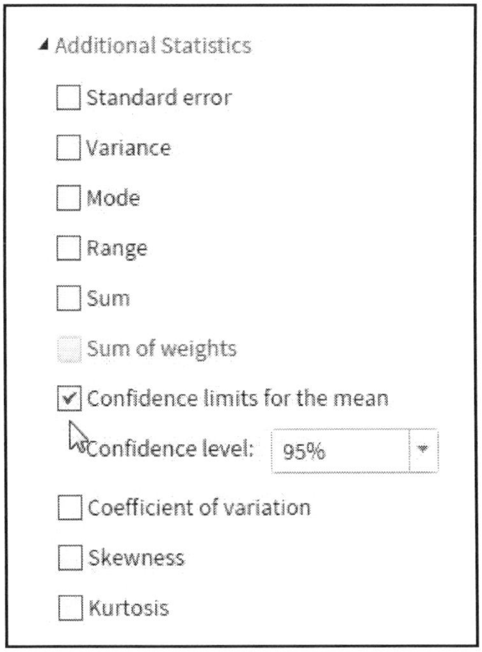

When you check the box for Confidence limits for the mean, the line below, labeled Confidence level, displays the default value of 95% for the CI. You can select other intervals, but 95% is the one most commonly used.

Finally, you can also select plots from the option list. Here you are requesting a histogram and box plot for the selected variables (Figure 7 below).

Figure 7: Requesting a Histogram and Box Plot

> ◢ PLOTS
>
> ☐ Histogram
>
> ☑ Histogram and box plot
>
>   Note: Plot is available when no classification variable is specified.
>
>   ☐ Add inset statistics

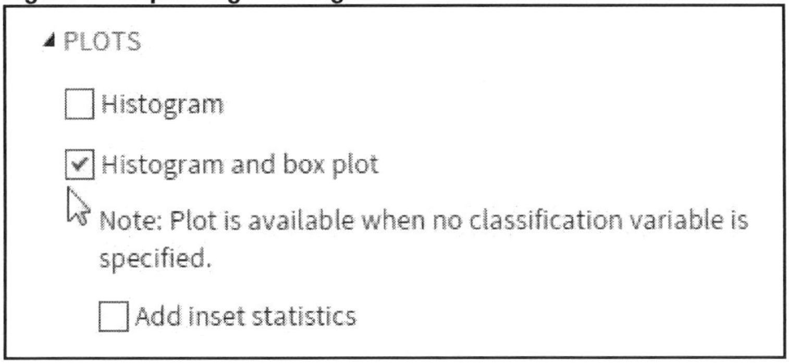

You are ready to click the Run Icon.

The first section of output shows basic statistics for the selected variables.

Figure 8: Descriptive Statistics for Selected Variables

Variable	Mean	Std Dev	Minimum	Maximum	Median	N	Lower 95% CL for Mean	Upper 95% CL for Mean
Height	64.8131847	3.5827074	51.5000000	76.5000000	64.5000000	5203	64.7158128	64.9105566
Weight	153.0866808	28.9154261	67.0000000	300.0000000	150.0000000	5203	152.3008087	153.8725528
Diastolic	85.3586101	12.9730913	50.0000000	160.0000000	84.0000000	5209	85.0062268	85.7109934
Systolic	136.9095796	23.7395964	82.0000000	300.0000000	132.0000000	5209	136.2647496	137.5544095

You see the mean, standard deviation, minimum, maximum, median, the number of nonmissing values, and the number of missing values for each of the analysis variables. The last two columns in the table represent the lower and upper 95% confidence interval for the mean.

The next section of output consists of a histogram and box-plot for each variable. To save space, only two histograms, one for Height and one for Systolic, are shown in the two figures that follow.

Figure 9: Histogram and Box Plot for Height

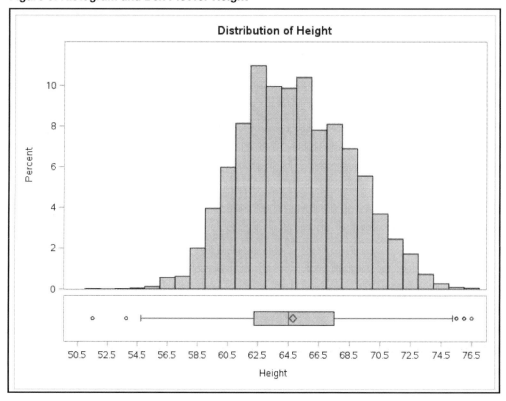

You can see that the distribution for Height is fairly symmetric and does not appear to have too many extreme values.

Figure 10: Histogram and Box Plot for Systolic

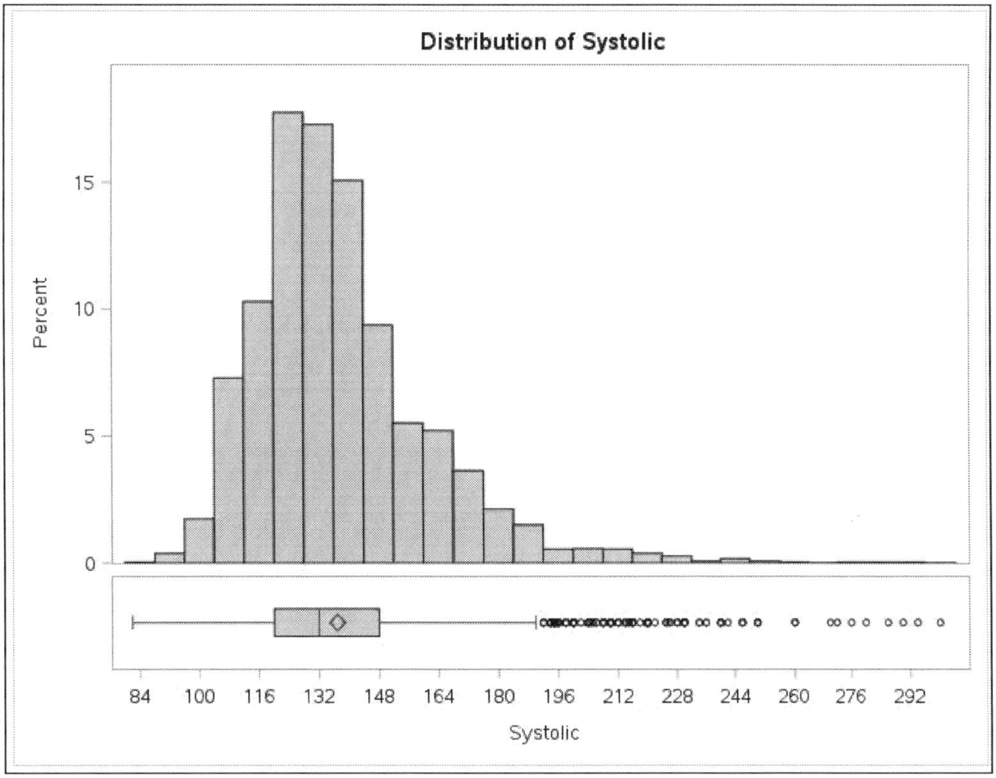

The histogram and box plot for Systolic was included to show a variable that is positively skewed, easily seen by the long tail on the right side of the histogram and by the outliers on the box plot (the circles on the right side of the plot). Notice that the mean, displayed as a diamond on the box plot is to the right of the median (displayed as a vertical line in the box), another indication that the data values are positively skewed.

Investigating the Distribution for Systolic Blood Pressure

At this point, you may want to further investigate the distribution of systolic blood pressure. One way to do this is to select Distribution Analysis from the list of Statistics tasks. Make sure that the Heart data set is selected on the DATA tab and Systolic is selected as the analysis variable. Click the OPTIONS tab to bring up the following menu:

Figure 11: Options for the Distribution Analysis Tab

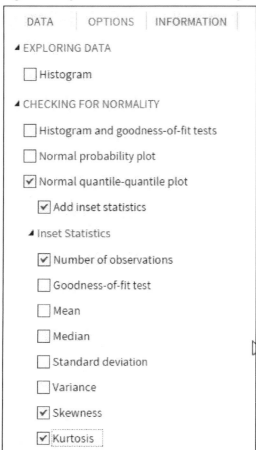

Because you have already produced a histogram from the Summary Statistics tab, you first want to deselect the box next to Histogram. Next, you have a choice of options for checking for normality. In this example, you are requesting a Q-Q (Quantile-Quantile) plot with added inset statistics. A Q-Q plot displays the quantiles of one distribution on the x-axis and the quantiles of another distribution on the y-axis. A quantile is the proportion or percent of a distribution that falls below a given value. For example, 25% of the data values will fall below the 25th percentile The Q-Q plot produced by SAS displays the quantiles of a theoretical distribution (in this case, a normal distribution) on the x-axis and the actual quantile for your sample distribution on the y-axis. You may recall that if you have normally distributed data, the Q-Q-plot will be a straight line.

Two popular statistics that quantify deviations from normality, Skewness and Kurtosis, are selected to be displayed in an inset box on the Q-Q-plot. Clicking the Run icon produces the following plot:

Figure 12: Q-Q-Plot for Systolic

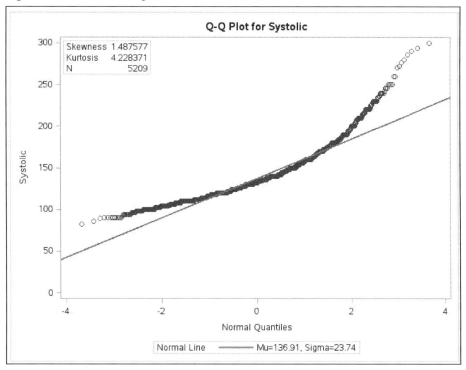

The straight line on the plot represents a normal distribution with the same mean and standard deviation as the variable Systolic. The circles on the plot represent values of systolic blood pressure from your sample data. At the bottom of the Q-Q plot, you see that the theoretical normal distribution has a mean (Mu) equal to 136.91 and a standard deviation (Sigma) equal to 23.74.

To help you understand this Q-Q plot, look at the right side of the plot. The circles above the straight line on this part of the plot indicate that your sample data includes values of systolic blood pressure that are higher (more extreme) than you would expect if the systolic blood pressures were normally distributed. This confirms the strong positive skewness that you saw in the histogram.

Values for Skewness and Kurtosis close to zero result from distributions that are close to normal. Positive values for skewness, as in this plot, indicate a positively skewed distribution (extreme values in the right tail). Positive values for kurtosis (as in this example) indicate both that the distribution is too peaked (leptokurtic) and that the tails are too heavy. Negative values for kurtosis indicate that the distribution is too flat (platykurtic) and that the tails are too light. Modern interpretation of kurtosis puts emphasis on the tails being too heavy or too light and deemphasizes the concepts of the distribution being too peaked or too flat.

When it is time to run statistical tests on systolic blood pressure and various categorical variables of interest, you may be concerned that the distribution for the variable Systolic deviates quite noticeably from a normal distribution. Because the sample size of the Heart data set is so large (over 5000), you may feel comfortable in running parametric tests such as *t* tests and ANOVA. Those types of decisions will be explored in later chapters that discuss inferential statistics.

Adding a Classification Variable in the Summary Statistics Tab

Suppose you want to compare the variable Height for males and females. You can go back to the Analysis variables section of the DATA tab and select Height and, in the box labeled Classification variables, add the variable Sex. Your DATA tab should now look like this:

Figure 13: Adding a Classification Variable

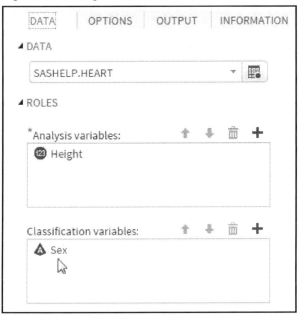

Under the Plots option, you can select a histogram and box plot to display distributions of Height for males and females (Figure 14 below).

Figure 14: Requesting Histograms and Box Plots

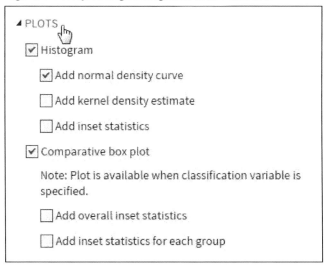

When you run this program, you see the following:

Figure 15: Histogram of Height by Sex

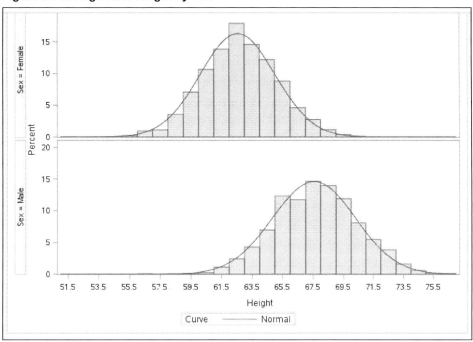

As expected, the center of the distribution for Sex=Male (bottom histogram) is shifted to the right compared to the distribution for Sex=Female.

You can see similar differences in the box plots (Figure 16 below).

Figure 16: Box Plots for Height and Sex

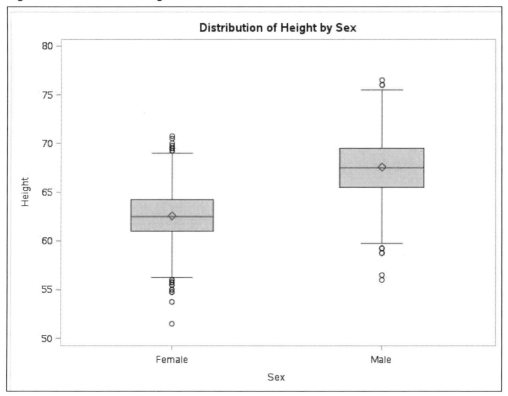

The box plots also show more outliers in the female distribution of Height compared to the male distribution. This may be partly due to the smaller interquartile range (the distance from the top to the bottom of the box) for the females compared to the males.

Describing Categorical Variables

Descriptive statistics for most categorical variables consist of frequency tables and bar charts. You may also want to display two-way tables to investigate relationships between two categorical variables (described in the next chapter).

The first step in generating frequency tables and bar charts is to double-click the One-Way Frequencies selection on the Statistics tab, as follows:

Figure 17: Selecting One-Way Frequencies

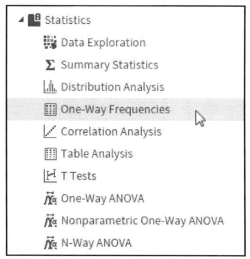

This brings up the DATA and OPTIONS tabs for this selection. For this example, three variables, Status, Sex, and Chol_Status were selected as analysis variables. Clicking the Options tab brings up the following screen:

Figure 18: DATA and OPTION for One-Way Frequencies

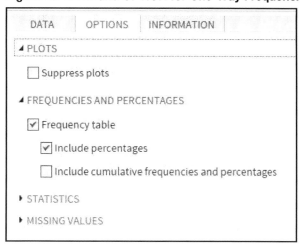

The box under Plots allows you to suppress plots. The default action is to produce plots (bar charts in this case). You also have options to include percentages and cumulative statistics. For this example, you want to include percentages and exclude cumulative frequencies and percentages. It's now time to click the Run icon.

To save space, only the output for Status is shown here.

Figure 19: Output from One-Way Frequencies (Variable Status)

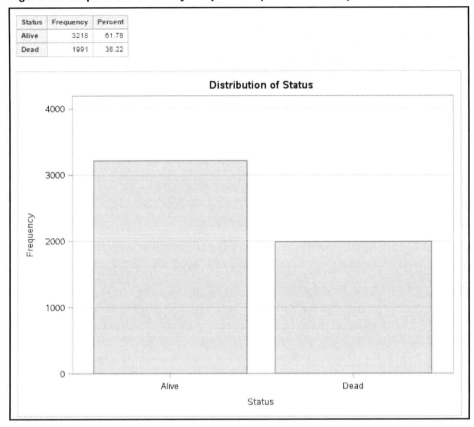

The frequency table shows the number of people in each category (Alive versus Dead) as well as a bar chart displaying the frequencies graphically.

By default, the option to produce plots produces two charts: one showing frequencies (counts), the other showing cumulative frequencies (displayed in Figure 20):

Figure 20: Cumulative Frequency Plot

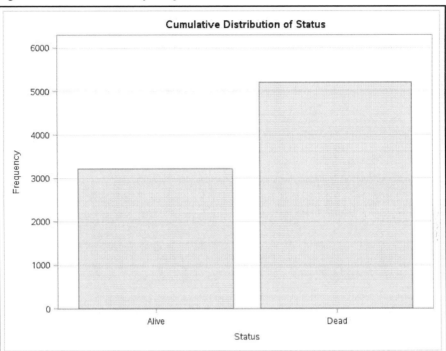

Editing the SAS Code Generated by the One-Way Frequencies Statistics Task

This is a good time to show you how to edit the SAS code produced by any of the SAS Studio tasks to customize the programs. Click the Code tab, and the SAS program generated by the One-Way Frequencies request appears in the right pane. It looks like this:

Figure 21: SAS Code Generated by the Request for One-Way Frequencies

```
proc freq data=SASHELP.HEART;
    tables Status Sex Chol_Status / nocum plots=(freqplot cumfreqplot);
run;
```

This program uses the FREQ (frequency) procedure to produce the frequency tables and plots for the One-Way Frequencies task. You provide a list of variables that you want to analyze in the TABLES statement. Following this list, you see a forward slash. A general rule in SAS procedures is that statement options (TABLES is considered a statement) are placed following a forward slash. Thus, NOCUM and PLOTS= are options that affect how the tables and charts appear. As you probably guessed, NOCUM is the instruction to omit cumulative statistics from the frequency table. Two plots, one a simple frequency plot and the other a cumulative frequency plot, are requested by the two plot requests (FREQPLOT and CUMFREQPLOT).

Let's modify this program in two ways: First, you want to add a customized title to the output; second, you want to omit the cumulative frequency plot. Here's how to do it:

The first step is to click the EDIT button at the top right of the code pane (see Figure 22 below).

Figure 22: Clicking the EDIT Button to Edit the Program

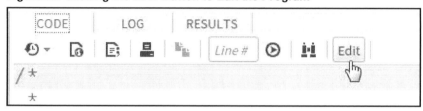

This action allows you to edit the task-produced program. To provide a customized title for the output, you use a TITLE statement. This consists of the keyword TITLE, followed by your title text, placed in single or double quotation marks. If any part of the title text contains a single quotation mark, be sure to use double quotation marks to enclose the title. Next, move the cursor to CUMFREQPLOT and delete it. The resulting program should now look like this:

Figure 23: The Edited Program

```
title "Frequencies on Data from the Health Data Set";
proc freq data=SASHELP.HEART;
    tables Status Sex Chol_Status / nocum plots=(freqplot);
run;
```

If you submit the program again, you will see your customized title and the bar chart showing cumulative frequencies will not be produced.

Conclusions

Before you conduct statistical tests on your data, it is a good idea to explore your data with the descriptive techniques (both tables and graphical output) described in this chapter. Knowing the shapes of distributions for continuous variables may affect your choice of statistical tests to perform. Frequency analysis will allow you to determine how many people (observations) belong to each category of a categorical variable. Both of these tasks also have the ability to uncover data errors.

Problems

5-1: One of the SASHELP data sets is called BMT (bone marrow transplant data). Compute summary statistics for the variable T (disease-free survival time). Remove the minimum and maximum value from the summary, and include the number of missing observations and the median. Also generate a histogram and box plot for this variable.

5-2: Using the same data set as problem 5-1, compute summary statistics for the variable T, broken down by the variable Group. Request a histogram and a comparative box plot.

5-3: Create a temporary SAS data set (call it BP) from the Excel workbook Blood_Pressure.xlsx. Using this data set, study the distribution of the two variables SBP and DBP. What does the Kolmogorov-Smirnov test tell you about these two variables? Include a request for a histogram and a Q-Q plot.

5-4: Using the BP data set from question 5-3, compute summary statistics for SBP with Drug as a classification variable. Add a request for a histogram and a comparative box plot.

5-5: Using the BP data set from question 5-3, compute frequencies for the two variables Drug and Gender. Omit cumulative statistics from the output. Suppress all plots.

Chapter 6: One-Sample Tests

Introduction

SAS Studio comes equipped with statistical tasks for just about any statistical query that you will need as a student or researcher.

You may have very little need to perform a one-sample test (of any kind), but let's start here anyway. First, this will show you how to navigate the various tabs that are common to all the statistical tasks. You will also see how to test some basic assumptions that need to be met before performing most parametric tests.

Performing a One-Sample t Test

A one-sample test is usually used when you have a null hypothesis that the mean of a sample is equal to a predetermined value. For example, suppose that you have several years of data on the weight of perch in a particular location. You wonder if the mean weight of these fish in the current season is different (perhaps lighter) from the mean weight computed from thousands of fish taken in the past several years.

For this imaginary situation, suppose that the mean weight of perch in your location, determined over several years, is 500 grams. You take a sample of the next 56 perch that are caught in this location and put the data into an Excel spreadsheet (called Perch.xlsx) as shown in Figure 1 below:

Figure 1: Perch Data in the File Perch.xlsx

	A	B	C
1	Weight	Height	Width
2	5.9	2.112	1.408
3	32	3.528	1.9992
4	40	3.824	2.432
5	51.5	4.5924	2.6316
6	70	4.588	2.9415
7	100	5.2224	3.3216
8	78	5.1992	3.1234
9	80	5.6358	3.0502
10	85	5.1376	3.0368
11	85	5.082	2.772
12	110	5.6925	3.555

Notice that the worksheet also contains the height and width of each fish. (You may want to work with these variables later.)

To perform a one-sample *t* test, your first step is to convert the Excel Workbook into a SAS data set. To make things simple, you placed the Perch.xlsx workbook in c:\SASUniversityEdition\myfolders, the location that was mapped to a location on your virtual machine called 'myfolders' when you installed SAS University Edition.

You use the Import Utility to import this data set. The steps are as follows:

1. Select the Tasks and Utilities tab and expand the Utilities options: It looks like this:

Figure 2: Expand the Utilities Options

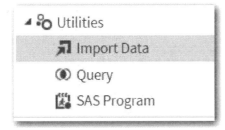

Double-click Import Data to see the screen below:

Figure 3: Select Import Data

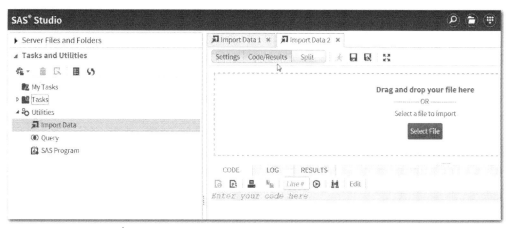

Remember, you can either click Select File or you can open the Server Files and Folders tab, locate the file Perch.xlsx, and drag it to the Drag and drop area. Because you used the Select File option in an earlier example, let's find the workbook under My folders and drag it over. It looks like this:

Figure 4: Using the Server Files and Folders Tab

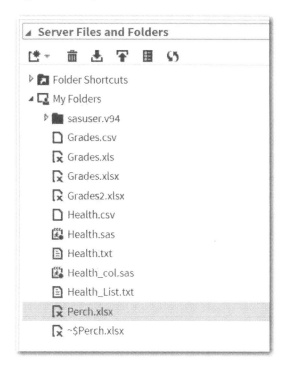

Place the cursor on Perch.xlsx, hold down the left mouse button, and drag it to the Drop and drag area. You decide to name the SAS data set Perch and place it in the Work library. You do this by clicking the Change button under the Output Data section of the screen (as shown in Figure 5 below):

Figure 5: Use the Change Button to Name the Output Data Set and Place it in the Work Library

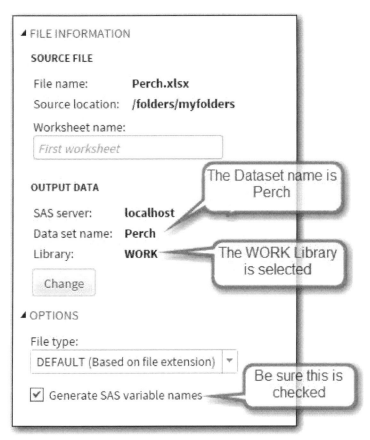

Make sure that the box next to Generate SAS variable names is checked (this is the default). This uses the column names from the spreadsheet to create SAS column names.

You are now ready to test if the mean weight of your 56 perch is different from the historical mean (that you can consider a population value) of 500. To start, select Tasks and Utilities ▶ Statistics ▶ t Tests,

Double-clicking *t* Tests brings up the following screen:

Figure 6: t Test Statistical Task

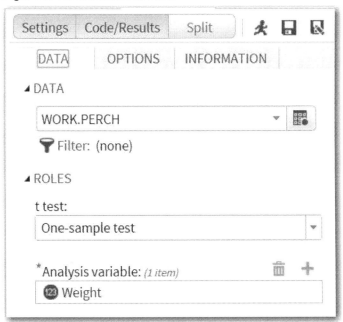

Select Work.Perch as the data set and make sure that One-sample test is selected in the Roles menu (this should be the first item in the pull-down list). Above the Analysis variable box, click the plus sign to bring up a list of numeric variables from the Perch data set. You will see Weight, Height, and Width listed. You can click Weight and then click OK or just double-click Weight. In either case, you will see Weight listed as the analysis variable.

Next, click the Options tab. This brings up the following:

Figure 7: Options for t Test

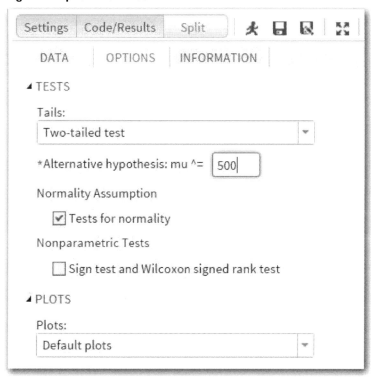

You select Two-tailed test and specify the alternative hypotheses as mu (µ) not equal to 500. You may be more familiar with stating that the null hypothesis is µ = 500 instead of the alternative hypothesis, but they are equivalent. Finally, check the box for Tests of normality and click the Run icon.

Figure 8: First Section of the One-sample t Test

Variable: Weight (Weight)

Tests for Normality				
Test	Statistic		p Value	
Shapiro-Wilk	W	0.816849	Pr < W	<0.0001
Kolmogorov-Smirnov	D	0.239184	Pr > D	<0.0100
Cramer-von Mises	W-Sq	0.810687	Pr > W-Sq	<0.0050
Anderson-Darling	A-Sq	4.362138	Pr > A-Sq	<0.0050

Figure 8 shows several methods for testing the null hypothesis that the distribution (of Weight in this example) is normally distributed. All of these tests reject the null hypothesis (at the α = .05

level). One of the assumptions for one- or two-sample *t* tests is that the data values come from a population of values that are normally distributed. At this point, you may be tempted to abandon the *t* test and choose a nonparametric alternative such as a sign test or a Wilcoxon rank sum test.

The decision whether to use a parametric test should not be determined solely by these tests of normality. You may recall that the central limit theorem states that the sampling distribution will be normally distributed, regardless of the population distribution, providing that n (the sample size) is sufficiently large. A sample size that is considered sufficiently large depends on the shape of the distribution of values. If the distribution is somewhat symmetrical, sufficiently large may be quite small (10 or 20). If the distribution is highly skewed, sufficiently large may be quite large. Before you decide to abandon the one-sample *t* test, you should take a look at the distribution of weights. The one-sample *t* test task produces both a histogram and a Q-Q plot to help you understand how your data values are distributed.

Figure 9, part of the output from the one-sample *t* test, shows a histogram with a normal distribution and a kernel distribution (a piecewise, smooth fit to the data) superimposed. Below the histogram, you also see a box plot. Although this is a skewed distribution, you may decide that with a sample size of 56, you can rely on the *t* test to decide if you should accept the alternative hypothesis (reject the null hypothesis). You probably want to check the nonparametric test results as well (you will see this later in this chapter).

Figure 9: Histogram and Box-Plot for Weight

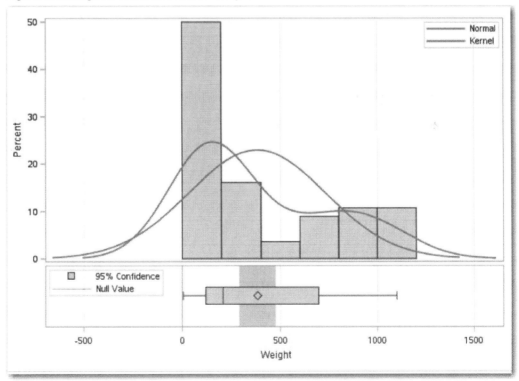

Another way to investigate deviations from a normal distribution is displayed in a Q-Q plot shown in Figure 10:

Figure 10: Q-Q Plot for Weight

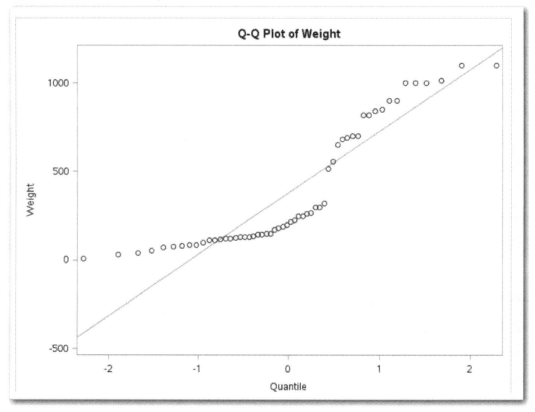

A Q-Q plot (stands for Quantile-Quantile) plot shows quantile values (think of these as z-values) on the x-axis and weight values on the y-axis. The closer the data points lie to the straight line on the plot, the closer the data values represent a normal distribution.

Let's go back and look at the results of the one-sample t test.

Figure 11: One-sample t Test results

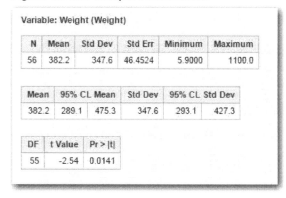

Variable: Weight (Weight)

N	Mean	Std Dev	Std Err	Minimum	Maximum
56	382.2	347.6	46.4524	5.9000	1100.0

Mean	95% CL Mean		Std Dev	95% CL Std Dev	
382.2	289.1	475.3	347.6	293.1	427.3

DF	t Value	Pr > |t|
55	-2.54	0.0141

The mean weight of your 56 perch was 382.2 with a standard deviation of 347.6. The 95% confidence limits (labeled 95% CL Mean in the output) indicate that you are 95% confident that the population mean from which you drew your sample is between these two values (289.1 and 475.3). Notice that the value 500 is not in this interval. Finally, you see a t value of -2.54 with a probability of .0141. If you set your α level at .05, you can now reject the null hypothesis and state that you believe that perch weights are lower than the historical value of 500.

Nonparametric One-sample Tests

Because the distribution of weights is significantly different from a normal distribution, you decide it would be a good idea to perform some nonparametric tests to confirm the conclusion from the one-sample *t* test. All you need to do is go back to the Options tab and request nonparametric tests. Because you have already run tests for normality and produced plots, you can uncheck the box next to Tests for normality and, in the menu for plots, select Suppress all plots. A portion of the Options screen is shown in Figure 12:

Figure 12: Option to Compute Nonparametric Tests

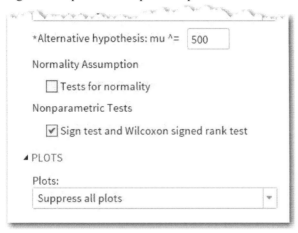

Click the Run icon to obtain the following:

Figure 13: Output from Nonparametric Tests

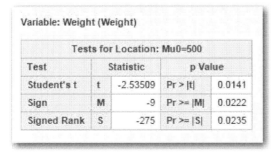

The same t table as shown in Figure 11 is produced (not shown) along with two nonparametric tests—the sign test and the signed rank test (the full name is the Wilcoxon Signed Rank test). Both of these tests produced *p*-values less than .05, backing up your conclusion based on the *t* test.

Conclusions

One of the advantages of running SAS Studio is the ease with which you can perform a large number of statistical tests. Yes, you still need to understand which tests to run and verify that the assumptions for those tests are satisfied. But once you have done this, getting your results is a few mouse clicks away.

Problems

6-1: Using the workbook Diabetes.xls, create a temporary SAS data set called Diabetes. Next, conduct a one-sample *t* test with the null hypothesis of Glucose = 200 (alternate hypothesis Glucose not equal 200). Include tests for normality and nonparametric tests.

6-2: Using the SASHELP data set Fish, test if the mean weight of Perch is equal to 500. To do this, click Filter on the Data tab and use the expression:

```
Species = 'Perch'
```

Include test for normality as well as histograms and Q-Q plots. After looking at these tests and plots, rerun the *t* test task requesting a Wilcoxon Rank sum test.

6-3: Using the SASHELP data set Heart, test if the mean weight is equal to 150. Include a test for normality and make sure that default plots is selected. Can you explain why the test is so highly significant when the mean weight is 153.1?

Chapter 7: Two-Sample Tests

Introduction

There are two classes of two-sample tests that you will see in this chapter. One is an unpaired *t* test (also called a *t* test for independent groups) that is used to compare means between two groups. The other type of two-sample *t* test is a paired *t* test. A common situation where a paired *t* test is performed is when each subject is measured twice, typically before and after some treatment. It can also be used when experimental units are paired on certain characteristics such as gender and age before the experiment and the variable of interest is the difference between values in each pair. Experimental units are often subjects, and that is the terminology subsequently used in the book.

As you saw with the one-sample *t* test, the two-sample statistical task also performs nonparametric tests, both for paired and unpaired situations.

Unpaired t Test (t Test for Independent Groups)

Let's start by using data from the SASHELP data set called Heart. This data set contains health and demographic information such as gender, health status, height, weight, blood pressure, and many risk factors such as cholesterol and smoking status. Suppose you wish to compare the variable Weight for men and women (variable Sex).

The first step is to open the t Test tab (the same process that you used for the one-sample *t* test):

Tasks and Utilities ▶ Statistics ▶ t Tests (double-click here)

This opens the following screen:

Figure 1: Data Tab for Two-Sample t Test

Data set Heart (in the SASHELP library) has been selected; a Two-sample *t* test has been selected from the pull-down list; the analysis variable is Weight; and the Group variable is Sex. It is important that the Group variable have only two possible values. If the Group variable has more than two values, you will see an error message in the log.

Before you run the *t* test, click the Options tab to bring up the following:

Figure 2: Options Tab for Two-Sample t Test

You are selecting a two-tailed test and verifying that the alternative hypothesis is that the two samples come from populations that have different means. For now, check the Tests for normality, leave the Nonparametric Tests unchecked, and accept the Default plots. You are now ready to run the test.

The first section of output is the requested normality tests (one for Females, the other for Males).

Figure 3: Normality Tests for Females and Males

Variable: Weight
Sex = Female

Tests for Normality				
Test	Statistic		p Value	
Kolmogorov-Smirnov	D	0.077525	Pr > D	<0.0100
Cramer-von Mises	W-Sq	4.91407	Pr > W-Sq	<0.0050
Anderson-Darling	A-Sq	29.30832	Pr > A-Sq	<0.0050

Variable: Weight
Sex = Male

Tests for Normality				
Test	Statistic		p Value	
Kolmogorov-Smirnov	D	0.033472	Pr > D	<0.0100
Cramer-von Mises	W-Sq	0.559512	Pr > W-Sq	<0.0050
Anderson-Darling	A-Sq	4.016874	Pr > A-Sq	<0.0050

All three tests for females and males show *p*-values below .05, meaning that you reject the null hypothesis that the distribution of weight for females and males is normally distributed. This is not surprising when you consider that there are over 2000 observations for both females and males. This means that even small deviations from a normal distribution will be significant (the test has high power because of the large sample size). You need to look at the actual distributions to decide if you can use a parametric test to test your hypothesis. The histogram and Q-Q plots appear at the end of the output (shown in Figure 5 and Figure 6).

The next portion of the output contains the means and other statistics on weight for females and males as well as the t- and *p*-values. This is shown in Figure 4 below:

Figure 4: Two-sample t Table

Method	Variances	DF	t Value	Pr > |t|
Pooled	Equal	5201	-36.20	<.0001
Satterthwaite	Unequal	5057.9	-36.34	<.0001

Equality of Variances				
Method	Num DF	Den DF	F Value	Pr > F
Folded F	2868	2333	1.08	0.0503

Variable: Weight

Sex	N	Mean	Std Dev	Std Err	Minimum	Maximum
Female	2869	141.4	26.2880	0.4908	67.0000	300.0
Male	2334	167.5	25.2907	0.5235	99.0000	276.0
Diff (1-2)		-26.0775	25.8454	0.7204		

Sex	Method	Mean	95% CL Mean		Std Dev	95% CL Std Dev	
Female		141.4	140.4	142.4	26.2880	25.6251	26.9865
Male		167.5	166.4	168.5	25.2907	24.5855	26.0379
Diff (1-2)	Pooled	-26.0775	-27.4899	-24.6652	25.8454	25.3582	26.3519
Diff (1-2)	Satterthwaite	-26.0775	-27.4843	-24.6708			

The mean weight for females and males was 141.4 and 167.5 pounds, respectively. The standard deviations were similar (26.2880 and 25.2907). You also see the 95% confidence limits for the means of females and males as well as the mean difference (labeled Diff (1-2)) and the 95% confidence limits for the difference. Note that there are two different confidence limits listed as well as two t- and p-values in the table. One set of values is computed under the assumption that the two groups have equal variance; the other set of values is computed under the assumption of unequal variance.

Which set of values should you use? There are different thoughts on how to approach this issue. The first, and probably the most common strategy, is to look at the F test at the bottom of the figure. The F test tests the equality of variances for the groups. The null hypothesis is that the variances are equal; the alternative hypothesis is that they are not equal. If the p-value for this test is less than .05, you would chose the t- and p- values under the assumption of unequal variances (the method used is labeled Satterthwaite in the table). If the p-value is greater than .05, you would use the values based on equal variances (labeled Pooled in the table).

Another train of thought says to decide before you conduct your study which assumption (equal or unequal variances) you think is reasonable. The idea behind this method is that collecting the data and making the decision based on the same data is somewhat circular. The good news is that for large samples the t test is very robust to the homogeneity of variance assumption, and the two p-values are usually close, even if there are relatively large differences in the variances.

Following rule one in this discussion, you see a p-value of .0503 for the test of homogeneity of variance and decide to use the pooled values in the table. You reject the null hypothesis that the populations from which you took the female and male weight samples have equal means. And you conclude that the female mean was less than the male mean.

Even though the histograms and Q-Q plots are displayed at the bottom of the results, you probably want to look at them before you examine and interpret the t table. These two plots are shown in the next two figures:

Figure 5: Histograms and Box Plots

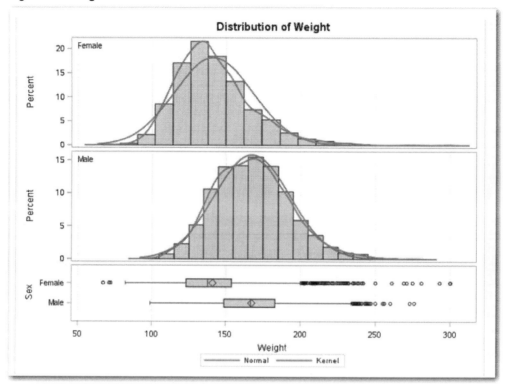

Figure 6: Q-Q Plots

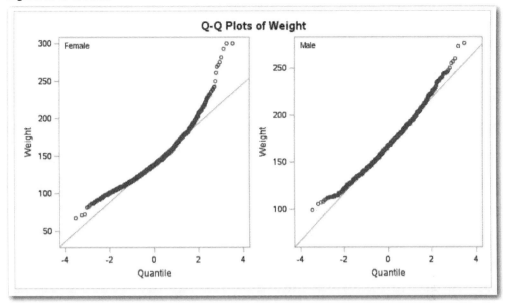

The histograms look quite close to normal while deviations from normality are a little more obvious in the Q-Q plots. However, with each group having a sample size of over 2000, you feel confident that using a *t* test is appropriate.

Nonparametric Two-sample Tests

If you want to compare two groups and you feel that the assumptions for a parametric test are not satisfied, the *t* test statistic task can also perform a Wilcoxon rank sum test, the nonparametric counterpart to the Student's *t* test.

To demonstrate how this works, let's use the SASHELP data set called Fish to demonstrate the Wilcoxon test. The Fish data set contains weights and several other variables on several species of fish. You decide to compare weights of two species: Roach and Pike. (Note: This author has never heard of a Roach fish.)

This example has two purposes: To demonstrate how to run and interpret a Wilcoxon Rank Sum test and how to filter rows in a table.

You start by double-clicking the *t* Test task as before. Next, on the Data tab, click Filter (as shown in Figure 7):

Figure 7: Filtering the Fish Table to Select Two Species

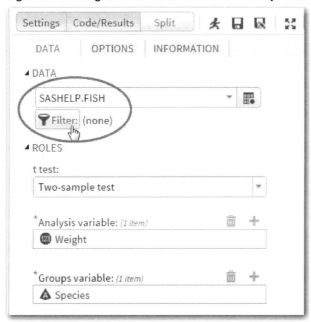

This opens the following screen:

Figure 8: Selecting Pike and Roach Species

Type the logical expression as seen in Figure 8. You can type logical expressions in the filter box such as the one to select the two fish species or other logical expressions such as Age < 30 or Height between 54 and 65. For those readers familiar with SQL, you can enter the same types of expressions that you would enter in a WHERE clause, except you do not include the word WHERE in the filter box.

Note: Because Species is a character variable, the values "Pike" and "Roach" must be in single or double quotation marks in the filter expression. For numeric variables, you do not place quotation marks around the numeric values.

You can undo a filter by clicking the small 'x' next to the filter text in the Data window.

You can now click the Run icon to display the results for the test of normality and see histograms for weights of the two selected fish species. The normality test results are shown in Figure 9, and the histograms are displayed in Figure 10.

Figure 9: Test of Normality for Two Species

Variable: Weight
Species = Pike

Tests for Normality				
Test	Statistic		p Value	
Shapiro-Wilk	W	0.821287	Pr < W	0.0040
Kolmogorov-Smirnov	D	0.267641	Pr > D	<0.0100
Cramer-von Mises	W-Sq	0.218639	Pr > W-Sq	<0.0050
Anderson-Darling	A-Sq	1.255384	Pr > A-Sq	<0.0050

Variable: Weight
Species = Roach

Tests for Normality				
Test	Statistic		p Value	
Shapiro-Wilk	W	0.932277	Pr < W	0.1708
Kolmogorov-Smirnov	D	0.176514	Pr > D	0.0986
Cramer-von Mises	W-Sq	0.102833	Pr > W-Sq	0.0968
Anderson-Darling	A-Sq	0.572359	Pr > A-Sq	0.1243

Figure 10: Distributions for Fish Weights

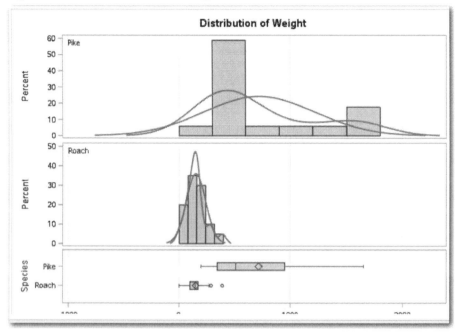

You need to pay closer attention to the distributions of weights because of the much smaller sample sizes for these two fish species (n=20 for Roach and n=17 for Pike). The tests for normality reject the null hypothesis that these weights for Pike come from a population that is normally distributed, and the histograms show a distribution that is not symmetric or normal.

Because of these results, you decide to run a Wilcoxon rank sum test. To do this, simply check the box labeled Wilcoxon Rank Sum Test on the Options tab, as shown in Figure 11:

Figure 11: Requesting the Wilcoxon Rank Sum Test

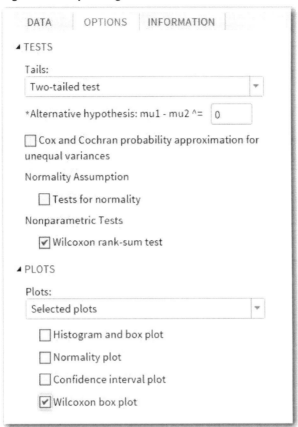

Because you have already seen the histograms, you can use the menu under Plots to select a Wilcoxon box plot (and deselect the other plots).

Click the Run icon to obtain the following:

Figure 12: Rank Sums for the Wilcoxon Rank Sum Test

Wilcoxon Scores (Rank Sums) for Variable Weight Classified by Variable Species					
Species	N	Sum of Scores	Expected Under H0	Std Dev Under H0	Mean Score
Roach	20	217.50	380.0	32.798983	10.875000
Pike	17	485.50	323.0	32.798983	28.558824
Average scores were used for ties.					

Figure 12 shows the sum of ranks for the two fish species. Here's how it works: You order all the fish weights (both species combined), from lowest to highest, giving then all ranks (the smallest is rank 1, the next smallest is rank 2, etc.). If there are two or more weights that are equal, you give them all the average rank. Finally, you add up the ranks for each species. In the figure above, you see this sum labeled Sum of Scores. If the null hypothesis is true, you would expect the sum of ranks to be about the same for both groups. Looking at the two histograms of weights, you see that, in general, the weights for Roach fish are lighter than the weights of the Pike. Therefore, you expect the sum of ranks for Roach to be lower than the sum of ranks for Pike. If the null hypothesis is true, large differences between the sum of ranks in the two samples are unlikely. That is the basis for computing a *p*-value for this test.

The next portion of the output shows you two ways to compute a *p*-value. One, useful for larger samples, is a z-test (with a correction for continuity); the other test, sometimes used for smaller samples, is a t approximation. In this table, both *p*-values are very small, and you can claim that Pike are heavier than Roach based on the population from which the samples were taken.

Figure 13: p-Values for the Wilcoxon Test

Wilcoxon Two-Sample Test	
Statistic	485.5000
Normal Approximation	
Z	4.9392
One-Sided Pr > Z	<.0001
Two-Sided Pr > |Z|	<.0001
t Approximation	
One-Sided Pr > Z	<.0001
Two-Sided Pr > |Z|	<.0001
Z includes a continuity correction of 0.5.	

Because you checked the box for a Wilcoxon box plot, you are presented with Figure 14:

Figure 14: Distribution of Wilcoxon Scores

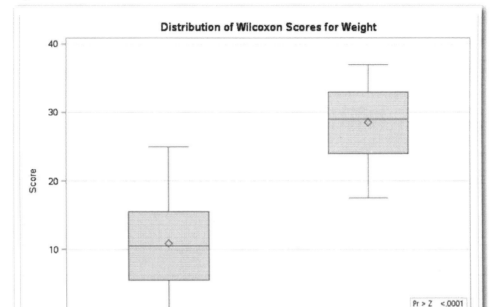

This plot shows the distribution of ranks for the two groups of fish. You can see that the Pike weights are given most of the larger rank values.

Paired t Test

The final section of this chapter describes a paired *t* test. This test is used when the situation either involves two values taken from each subject (such as a score taken before and after a subject is treated) or two subjects who are paired on one or more characteristics. Then one is randomly assigned to one treatment and the second to the other treatment

To demonstrate a paired *t* test, you can use data from a small study designed to show if a half hour of yoga can lower a subject's heart rate. Ten subjects had their heart rate measured before and after the yoga session, and the results were entered into an Excel workbook called Yoga.xlsx.

This workbook was saved in the folder c:\SASUniversityEdition\myfolders. Figure 15 (below) shows the original spreadsheet:

Figure 15: Spreadsheet Containing Before and After Heart Rates

	A	B	C
118			
1	Subj	Before	After
2	1	78	74
3	2	68	68
4	3	76	70
5	4	58	57
6	5	83	73
7	6	80	77
8	7	69	61
9	8	77	76
10	9	77	72
11			

The Import Utility under the Tasks and Utilities tab was used to convert the workbook into a SAS data set called Yoga that was placed in the Work library. The next step is to double-click the t Test tab and enter the appropriate information on the Data tab. The data set name is

WORK.Yoga. A paired *t* test is selected from the menu, and the two variables, Before and After, are entered as the Group1 and Group 2 variables. (See Figure 16 below.)

Figure 16: Data Tab for Paired t Test

It's time to run the procedure (you are leaving all the defaults on the Options tab). Here are the results:

Figure 17: Test for Normality for Difference Scores

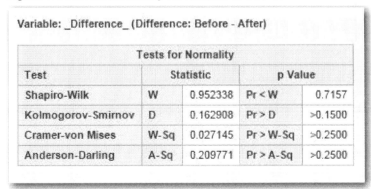

All of the test for normality are not significant. You should not interpret this to mean that the difference scores are normally distributed. With such a small sample (10 subjects), it would take large deviations from a normal distribution to reject the null hypothesis at the .05 level. You will need to look at the histogram (or a Q-Q plot) to help decide if a parametric test is reasonable.

The next section of the output shows the t table. You see that the mean difference is 4.222, the t value is 3.74, and the *p*-value is .0057. Because the mean difference is positive and the difference score was computed as the before value minus the after value, you can conclude that the yoga session helped reduce heart rate (at the .05 level).

Figure 18: Statistics, t- and p-Values

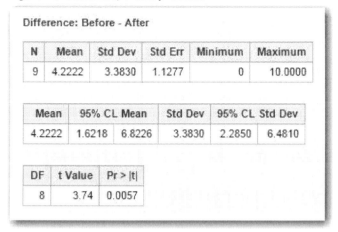

Difference: Before - After

N	Mean	Std Dev	Std Err	Minimum	Maximum
9	4.2222	3.3830	1.1277	0	10.0000

Mean	95% CL Mean		Std Dev	95% CL Std Dev	
4.2222	1.6218	6.8226	3.3830	2.2850	6.4810

DF	t Value	Pr > |t|
8	3.74	0.0057

The final section of the output shows a histogram for the difference scores. Although it doesn't look too much like a normal distribution. It is fairly symmetric and with a sample size of 10, you decide that a *t* test is appropriate.

Figure 19: Histogram of Difference Scores

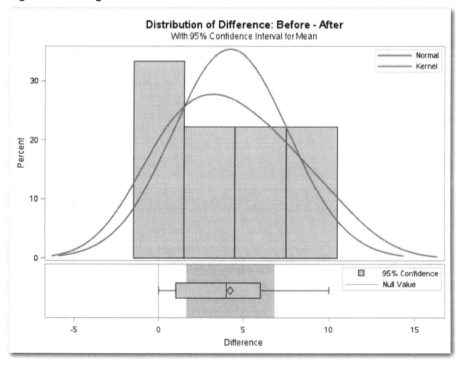

If you have any doubts, you should rerun the analysis using a nonparametric test such as the Wilcoxon Signed Rank test. This is accomplished by checking the box on the Options tab that requests this test. (Actually, the option runs both a Sign test and a Wilcoxon Signed Rank test.) Although not shown here, these two nonparametric tests both show a significant difference at the .05 level.

Conclusions

You have seen that the *t* test statistics task can perform one-sample *t* tests as well as two-sample paired and unpaired tests. For each of these tests, one or more nonparametric alternatives are provided. Because one of the assumptions for all of the *t* tests is that the data values are normally distributed (or close to it, depending on the sample size), the task provides you with test of normality as well as histograms and Q-Q plots. One final thought: Do not simply look at the *p*-values from the normality tests. Doing so often results in incorrect decisions. When sample sizes are large, the tests for normality are often significant. When sample sizes are small, they are rarely significant. And, it is with small samples that deviations from normality are most important.

Problems

7-1: Using the SAS data set Diabetes from problem 6-1, compute a two-sample *t* test that compares Glucose from two of the three Diet_Drinks values (omit Diet_Drinks = 'Sometimes'). Hint: Your filter statement should read:

```
Diet_Drinks ne 'Sometimes'
```

7-2: Using the SAS data set Diabetes from problem 6-1, compute a two-sample *t* test that compares Glucose between the two values for the variable Insulin (1=yes uses insulin, 0=does not use insulin). Add a test for normality for Glucose.

7-3: (advanced) You have measured the heart rate of 12 subjects before and after they have each drunk a cup of coffee. The values are as follows:

```
Coffee and Heart Rate Data

 Subj    Before     After

  1        74         89
  2        78         62
  3        72         77
  4        70         78
  5        68         76
  6        81         79
  7        55         84
  8        68         68
  9        72         82
 10        61         76
 11        74         79
 12        70         79
```

Create a SAS data set (call it Coffee) from this data either by entering it into Excel and using the Import utility or by writing a DATA step (if you feel confident in your SAS programming ability). Once you do this, run a paired *t* test comparing the Before and After values.

7-4: Use the Excel workbook Coffee_HR.xls to create a SAS data set called Coffee_HR. This data set will contain the variables Subj, Group (Coffee or Placebo), and HR (heart rate). Conduct a two-sample *t* test to compare heart rates between the Coffee and Placebo groups.

Chapter 8: Comparing More Than Two Means (ANOVA)

Introduction

When you want to compare means in a study where there are three or more groups, you cannot use multiple *t* tests. In the old days (even before my time!), if you had three groups (let's call them A, B, and C), you might perform *t* tests between each pair of means (A versus B, A versus C, and B versus C). With four groups, the situation gets more complicated; you would need six *t* tests (A versus B, A versus C, A versus D, B versus C, B versus D, and C versus D). Even though no one does multiple *t* tests anymore, it is important to understand the underlying reason why this is not statistically sound.

Suppose you are comparing four groups and performing six *t* tests. Also, suppose that the null hypothesis is true, and all the means come from populations with equal means. If you perform each *t* test with α set at .05, there is a probability of .95 that you will make the correct decision—that is, to fail to reject the null hypothesis in each of the six tests. However, what is the probability that you will reject at least one of the six null hypotheses? To spare you the math, the answer is about .26 (or 26% if that is easier to think about). This is called an "experiment-wise" type I error. Remember, a type I error is when you reject the null hypothesis (claim the samples come from populations with different means—"the drug works")—when you shouldn't. So, instead of your chance of reporting a false positive result being .05, it is really .26.

To prevent this problem, statisticians came up with a single test, called analysis of variance (abbreviated ANOVA). The null hypothesis is that all the means come from populations with the same mean; the alternative is that there is at least one pair of means that are different. You either reject or fail to reject the null hypothesis, and there is one *p*-value associated with the test. If you reject the null hypothesis, you can then investigate pairwise differences using methods that control the experiment-wise type I error.

Performing a One-Way Analysis of Variance

Once again, let's start by using data from the SASHELP data set called Heart. This time you want to see if there are differences in the weight for each of the three levels of cholesterol (High, Borderline, and Desirable).

You start by choosing the task One-Way ANOVA from the statistics task list. This brings up the following screen:

Figure 1: Data Tab for One-Way ANOVA

The data set SASHELP.Heart was selected by clicking the icon to the right of the Data rectangle. The dependent and categorical variables (Weight and Chol_Status, respectively) have also been selected. You may be more familiar with the term independent variable instead of categorical variable. In this context, they mean the same thing.

Once you have completed the Data screen, click the Options tab to see the following:

Figure 2: Options for One-Way ANOVA (top portion)

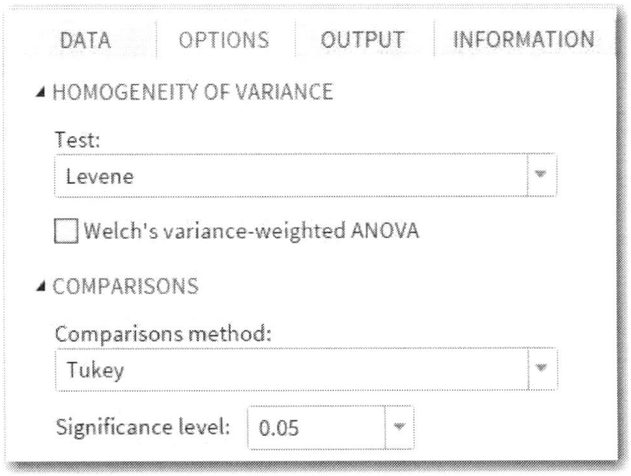

One of the assumptions for performing an analysis of variance is that the variances in each of the groups are equal. The Levene test is one test that is used to determine if this assumption is reasonable. If this test is significant, you may choose to ignore it if the differences are not too large. (ANOVA is said to be robust to the assumption of equal variance, especially if the sample sizes are similar.) If you want to account for unequal variances, click the box for Welch's variance-weighted ANOVA.

Multiple comparisons are methods that we use in order to determine which pairs of means differ. There are several choices for these tests. The default is Tukey, a popular choice. Later in this chapter, you will see another multiple comparison test called SNK (Student-Newman-Keuls). You probably want to leave the significance level at .05.

Further down on the Options tab are plot options (Figure 3): You can accept the default plots or request all the plots as shown here. You also have a choice to display the diagnostic plots as a panel (several smaller graphs displayed in a grid) or as individual plots (the selection here). Finally, because the SASHELP.Heart data set has over 5,000 rows, you need to remove the 5,000-point default limit on plots to have then display correctly.

Figure 3: Options for One-Way ANOVA (Bottom Portion)

It's time to run the procedure. Click the Run icon to produce the tables and graphs.

The first section of output displays class-level information. Don't ignore this! Make sure that the number of levels is what you expected (data errors can cause the program to believe there are more levels). Also, pay attention to the number of observations read and used. This is important because any missing values on either the dependent (Weight) or categorical (Chol_Status) variable will result in that observation being omitted from the analysis. A large proportion of missing values in the analysis may lead to bias—subjects with missing values may be different in some way from subjects without missing values (i.e., missing values may not be random).

Figure 4: Class-Level Information

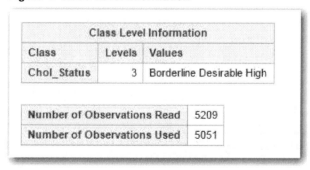

You see three levels for Chol_Status (as expected) and a relatively small number of subjects with missing values.

It's time to look at your ANOVA table (Figure 5 below):

Figure 5: ANOVA Table

Dependent Variable: Weight

Source	DF	Sum of Squares	Mean Square	F Value	Pr > F
Model	2	42864.375	21432.188	25.90	<.0001
Error	5048	4176597.649	827.377		
Corrected Total	5050	4219462.024			

R-Square	Coeff Var	Root MSE	Weight Mean
0.010159	18.79164	28.76416	153.0689

Source	DF	Type I SS	Mean Square	F Value	Pr > F
Chol_Status	2	42864.37515	21432.18758	25.90	<.0001

Source	DF	Type III SS	Mean Square	F Value	Pr > F
Chol_Status	2	42864.37515	21432.18758	25.90	<.0001

You can look at the F test and *p*-values in the ANOVA table, but you must remember that you also need to look at the several other parts of the output to determine if the assumptions for the test are satisfied. You will see in the diagnostic tests that follow that the ANOVA assumptions were satisfied, so let's go ahead and see what conclusions you can draw from the ANOVA table and the tables that follow.

Notice that the model has 2 degrees of freedom (because there were 3 levels of the independent variable). The mean squares for the model and error terms tell you the between-group variance and the within-group variance. The ratio of these two variances, the F value, is 25.90 with a corresponding *p*-value of less than .0001. A result such as this is often referred to as "highly significant." Remember, the term "significant" means that there is a low probability that one or more of the pairwise differences occurred by chance. It doesn't necessarily mean that the differences are significant in the common usage of the word, that is, important.

The next several plots are intended to help you decide if the ANOVA assumptions were satisfied and to graphically show you information about the 3 means and the distribution of scores in each of the 3 groups.

Note: The figures shown below were selected from a larger set of plots produced by the one-way ANOVA task.

The plot shown in Figure 6 shows the residuals (the differences between the mean of each group and each individual score) in that group. There are actually two residual plots produced by the one-way task. One (not shown) displays the residuals as actual scores (weights in this example). The one selected here displays the residuals as t scores (the number of standard deviations above or below the mean of the group). Both plots look very similar. You also see the predicted values (means of each group) shown on the x-axis.

Figure 6: Residual Plot

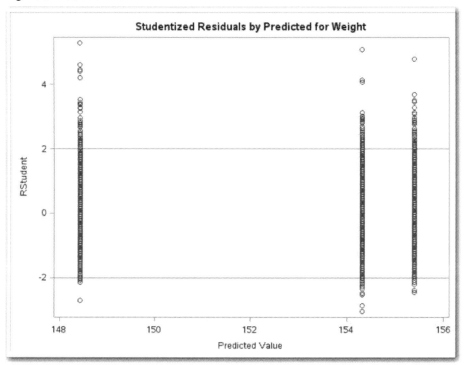

One of the assumptions for running a one-way ANOVA is that the errors (the residuals are estimates of these errors) are normally distributed. You have seen Q-Q plots earlier in this book, so you remember that data values that are normally distributed appear as a straight line on a Q-Q plot. The plot shown in Figure 7 shows small deviations from a straight line, but not enough to invalidate the analysis.

Figure 7: Q-Q Plot for Residuals

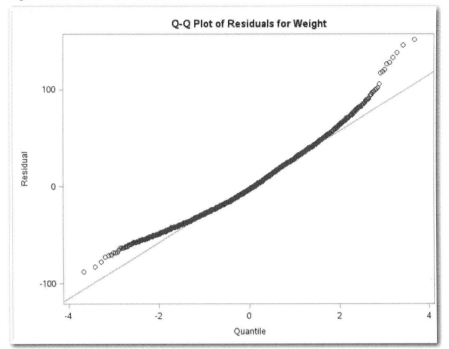

The residuals are also displayed as a histogram (see Figure 8):

Figure 8: Histogram for Residuals

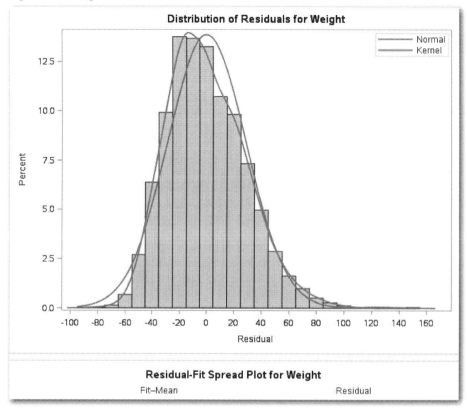

To graphically display the distribution of weights in the 3 groups, the one-way ANOVA task produces a box plot (Figure 9). The line in the center of the box represents the median, and the small diamond represents the mean. Notice that the means, as well as the medians, of the three groups are not very different. Why then were the results so highly significant? The reason is the large (over 5,000) sample size. Large sample sizes give you high power to see even small differences.

Figure 9: Box Plot for Weight by Cholesterol Level

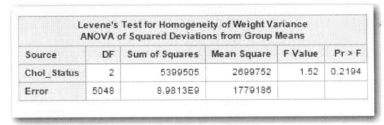

Figure 10 shows the results for Levin's test of homogeneity of variance. Here, the null hypothesis is that the variances are equal. Because the *p*-value is .2194, you do not reject the null hypothesis of equal variance.

Figure 10: Levin's Test for Homogeneity of Variance

Levene's Test for Homogeneity of Weight Variance ANOVA of Squared Deviations from Group Means					
Source	DF	Sum of Squares	Mean Square	F Value	Pr > F
Chol_Status	2	5399505	2699752	1.52	0.2194
Error	5048	8.9813E9	1779186		

Figure 11 show the means and standard deviations for the three groups.

Figure 11: Group Means and Standard Deviations

Level of Chol_Status	N	Weight	
		Mean	Std Dev
Borderline	1860	154.318280	28.5982126
Desirable	1403	148.431219	29.6364336
High	1788	155.408277	28.2367277

Because this is a one-way model, the least square means shown in Figure 12 are equal to the means in the previous figure. In unbalanced models with more than one factor, this may not be the case.

Below the table showing the three means, you see *p*-values for all of the pairwise differences. Each of the three cholesterol groups in the top table in the figure has what is labeled as the LSMEAN Number. In the table of *p*-values, the LSMEAN number is used to identify the groups. The intersection of any two groups displays the *p*-value for the difference. For example, group 1 (Borderline) and group 2 (Desirable) show a *p*-value of less than .0001. The *p*-value for the difference of Borderline (1) and High (3) is .4869 (not significant).

Figure 12: Least Square Means

Least Squares Means
Adjustment for Multiple Comparisons: Tukey-Kramer

Chol_Status	Weight LSMEAN	LSMEAN Number
Borderline	154.318280	1
Desirable	148.431219	2
High	155.408277	3

Least Squares Means for effect Chol_Status
Pr > |t| for H0: LSMean(i)=LSMean(j)

Dependent Variable: Weight

i/j	1	2	3
1		<.0001	0.4869
2	<.0001		<.0001
3	0.4869	<.0001	

Figure 13 shows a very clever way to display pairwise differences. At the intersection of any two groups, you see a diagonal line representing a 95% confidence interval for the difference between the two group means. If the interval crosses the main diagonal line (that represents no difference), the two group means are not significantly different at the .05 level. To make this clearer, significant differences are shown in blue and non-significant differences are shown in red.

Figure 13: Pairwise Comparison of Means

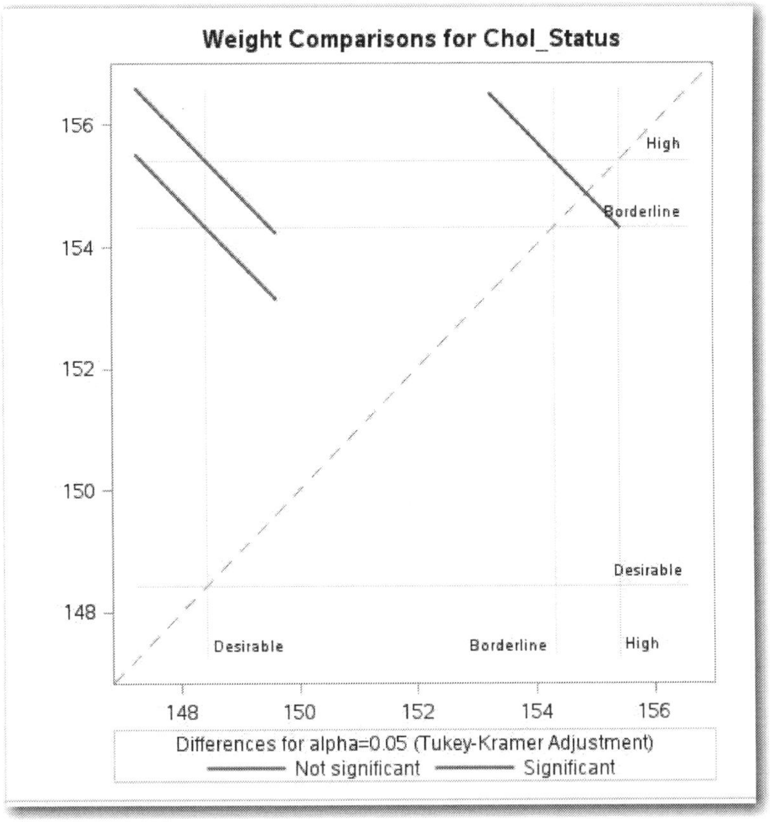

All of the previous figures were generated by the choices that you made in the Data and Options tabs. The last figure (below) shows an alternative method of determining pairwise differences, called the Student-Newman-Keuls test (also referred to in some texts as just Newman-Keuls). The SNK (the abbreviation for this test) test is similar to the Tukey test in that it shows group means and which pairs of means are different at the .05 level. The Tukey test has the advantage of computing *p*-values for each pair of means as well as a confidence interval for the differences. The SNK test can do neither of these two things but has a slightly higher power to detect differences. The SNK display shows the three means in order from highest to lowest. To the left of the means is a column labeled SNK Grouping. Any two means that have the same grouping letter are not significantly different. You can see here that the mean weights for the cholesterol groups High and Borderline are not significantly different (they both have As in the grouping column). The mean weight for the Desirable group is significantly different from the other two groups (it has a B in the grouping column).

Figure 14: Student-Newman-Keuls Pairwise Comparisons

SNK Grouping	Mean	N	Chol_Status
A	155.4083	1788	High
A			
A	154.3183	1860	Borderline
B	148.4312	1403	Desirable

Means with the same letter are not significantly different.

Performing a Nonparametric One-Way Tests

If you feel that the distribution assumptions are not satisfied by your data, another statistical task, Nonparametric One-Way analysis, provides a host of alternate tests. To demonstrate this, let's go back to the SASHELP data set called Fish and compare the weights of three species of fish.

This exercise also provides you with a demonstration of an alternate way of filtering data. Rather than creating the filter directly in the statistics task as you did in Chapter 7, you can use a Filter Data task under the list of Data tasks. To this end, let's add Bream to the weight comparison of Pike and Roach. You may find this method easier than having to write your own filter expression—you create a filter by choosing items in menus.

In the navigation pane, from the Task list, select Data ▶ Filter Data. This brings up the following:

Figure 15: Creating a Filter with a Data Task

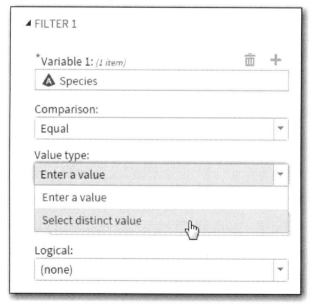

You selected Species as the first variable, Equal as the comparison, and Select a distinct value as the Value type. This brings up a list of all the species in the Fish data set. It looks like this:

Figure 16: Selecting a Distinct Value for Species

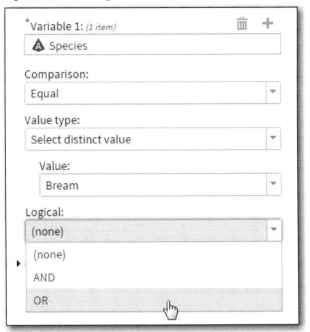

Because you want to add Roach and Pike to this list, select OR as your logical operator. This enables you to repeat the filtering process adding the other two species to the data set. Finally, on the tab labeled Output, select a name for your output data set (Three_Fish was used in this example), and select which variables you want in the output data set (Species and Weight were selected here). Now, run the task.

This is certainly more tedious than simply writing a WHERE clause as you did in Chapter 7, but, by presenting you with lists of species, it helps avoid spelling or syntax errors.

It's time to run the Nonparametric One-Way Statistic task. The opening screen looks like this:

Figure 17: Opening Screen of the Nonparametric One-Way Task

The data set Three_Fish is selected, along with Weight as the Dependent variable and Species as the Classification variable. For this example, you are using all the default values except for a request for multiple comparisons that you decided to check (see Figure 18 below):

Figure 18: Requesting a Multiple Comparison Test

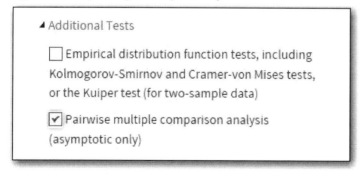

You are ready to run the analysis. Below are selected portions of the output:

Figure 19: Wilcoxon Rank Sums and Kruskal-Wallis ANOVA Table

Wilcoxon Scores (Rank Sums) for Variable Weight Classified by Variable Species					
Species	N	Sum of Scores	Expected Under H0	Std Dev Under H0	Mean Score
Bream	34	1580.00	1224.0	86.852273	46.470588
Roach	20	224.50	720.0	78.206158	11.225000
Pike	17	751.50	612.0	74.192876	44.205882
Average scores were used for ties.					

Kruskal-Wallis Test	
Chi-Square	40.2791
DF	2
Pr > Chi-Square	<.0001

Looking at the results of the Kruskal-Wallis test, you decide that the fish weights are not all equal (p <.0001). Box plots are shown next:

Figure 20: Box Plots for Fish Weights

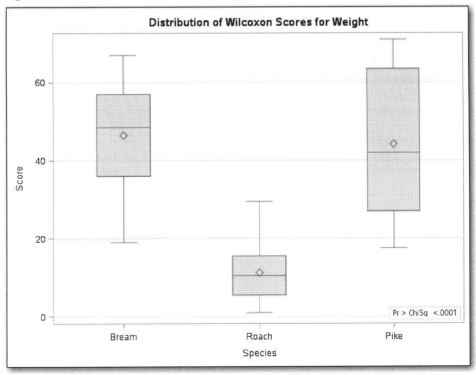

It looks like Roach are much lighter than either Bream or Pike. However, to determine which pairs of fish are unequal, look at the final piece of output (Figure 21) to see the *p*-values for each of the pairs. You see that the comparisons Bream versus Roach and Roach versus Pike are significantly different while the comparison of Bream versus Pike is not. Exactly what you would have guessed from the box plot.

Figure 21: Pairwise Comparisons

Pairwise Two-Sided Multiple Comparison Analysis			
Dwass, Steel, Critchlow-Fligner Method			
Variable: Weight			
Species	Wilcoxon Z	DSCF Value	Pr > DSCF
Bream vs. Roach	5.9671	8.4388	<.0001
Bream vs. Pike	0.4599	0.6504	0.8900
Roach vs. Pike	-4.9544	7.0066	<.0001

Conclusions

You have seen how to conduct a one-way analysis of variance as well as a Kruskal-Wallis nonparametric test. You have also seen ways to determine if the two assumptions for a one-way ANOVA (normally distributed data and homogeneity of variance) are met. Finally, you saw an alternative way to filter data using the Filter Data task.

Problems

8-1: Starting with the workbook Blood_Pressure.xls, create a temporary SAS data set called BP. Use this data set to perform a one-way ANOVA, testing the three drugs' effects on SBP (systolic blood pressure). What is the overall *p*-value for the test? Using the Tukey (default) method of multiple comparisons, what do you conclude about the three drug levels (Placebo, Drug A, and Drug B)?

8-2: Repeat problem 8-1, except start with the SAS data set Blood_Pressure.sas7bdat, which is located in the folder c:\SASUniversityEdition\myfolders\Problems. You may need to review the instructions describing the problem sets to see how to create a library.

8-3: Starting with the Diabetes.xls workbook, create a SAS data set called Diabetes. Test if there is a relationship between how often a person drinks diet drinks (variable Diet_Drinks) and the glucose level. What is the overall *p*-value for the ANOVA; test if there are any pairwise differences. If so, what are they, and what are the *p*-values?

8-4: Repeat problem 8-3, except request the SNK (Student-Newman-Keuls) multiple comparison test. Because this test has a slightly high power to detect group differences, is the difference between the levels Rarely and Sometimes significant (at the .05 level)?

8-5: Using the SASHELP data set BMT, test if the T values are different for each of the three groups. What is the overall *p*-value, and which groups, if any, are significantly different at the .05 level?

8-6: You have measured the left ventricular ejection fraction (LVEF) on three groups of subjects with congestive heart failure (CHF). LVEF is the percentage of blood volume that is pumped from the left ventricle with each contraction. The three groups represent 1) Placebo, 2) Calcium channel blocker, and 3) Lasix. The experiment resulted in the following:

```
Placebo: 55 58 62 48 57 57 80 40 55 52
Calcium: 57 65 55 78 57 84 72 80 78 81
Lasix:   60 60 65 67 48 62 64 70 57 40
```

Run the program below to create the CHF data set. The variables in this data set are Subj, Group (Placebo, Calcium, or Lasix), and LVEF. There will be a short explanation following the program:

```
1.  data CHF;
2.     do Group = 'Placebo','Calcium','Lasix';
3.        do Subj = 1 to 10;
4.           input LVEF @@;
5.           output;
6.        end;
7.     end;
8.  datalines;
    55 58 62 48 57 57 80 40 55 52
    57 65 55 78 57 84 72 80 78 81
    60 60 65 67 48 62 64 70 57 40
    ;
```

The program starts with a DATA statement (1). Line 2 demonstrates a DO loop with character values. Group is first set to 'Placebo'. Then another DO loop creates a Subj variable with values from 1 to 10 (line 3). For each combination of Group and Subj, you read in a value for LVEF. The @@ on line 4 enables you to place several observations on a single line of data. Without the @@ on the INPUT statement, the program would go to a new line of data for each input. You finish each DO loop with an END statement. Finally, in line 8, you see a DATALINES statement. This enables you to enter the data value directly in the SAS program, avoiding the effort of first creating a text file and then using an INFILE statement to tell the program where to read the data values.

Run a one-way ANOVA comparing LVEF for each of the three groups. Include a test for Tukey multiple comparisons.

Chapter 9: N-Way ANOVA

Introduction

You can construct ANOVA models with more than one independent variable. One of the most popular models is called a factorial model. In a factorial model, you compute variances for each independent variable as well as interaction terms. For example, if you want to investigate how race and smoking status affect a baby's birth weight, you could construct a model that looks at race (adjusted for smoking status), smoking status (adjusted for race), and each combination of race and smoking status.

The statistics task N-Way ANOVA helps you analyze factorial models as well as more advanced models that involve crossing and nesting.

Performing a Two-Way Analysis of Variance

One of the data sets in the SASHELP library is called Bweight (stands for birth weight). This fairly large data set contains birth weights for 50,000 babies, along with several variables believed to be related to birth weight, such as race (coded as black or not black), mother's smoking status (smoking or non-smoking), and marital status.

Selecting a Random Sample

Because this is such a large data set, you will see how to take a random subset using one of the Data tasks. In practice, you would use all the data in such a data set, but there are two reasons to consider a subset: First, you will see how to use the Random Subset task; second, using a smaller data set will reduce processing time. (If you are not interested in how to select a random sample, feel free to skip this section and jump right to the two-way ANOVA). Let's get started with the random selection:

Expand the Data task and double-click Select Random Sample. Select Tasks and Utilities ▶ Select Random Sample. This brings up the following screen:

Figure 1: Selecting a Random Sample

Select SASHELP.Bweight as the Data selection, and check the box to include all of the variables from the original data set. You also get to name the output data set (see Figure 2).

Figure 2: Name Your Random Sample

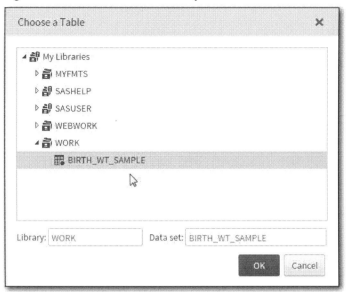

You see that the name Birth_Wt_Sample has been selected and will be located in the WORK library. Now click the Options tab to specify the sampling method and the size of the random sample and what is called a seed number (see Figure 3):

Figure 3: Requesting a 25% Sample and a Fixed Seed

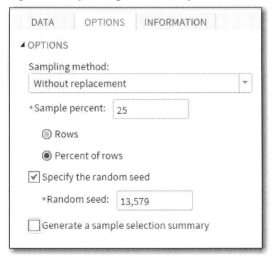

The most common sampling method is to select the sample without replacement. This ensures that an observation cannot be selected more than once. You can specify the size of the random sample in two ways: (1) You can enter the number of rows you want in the sample; or (2) you can specify what percentage of the rows in the original data set you want in the sample.

The last decision you need to make concerning the random sample is whether to specify a random seed. If you leave the option to specify a random seed unchecked, the program will generate a random series of random numbers. If you check this option, the program will generate a repeatable series of random numbers. This may sound confusing, so here is a more detailed explanation:

To generate random numbers, the random-number generator needs what is called a seed, a number that the random number generator uses to start the random sequence. If you do not specify this seed number, the program uses a number taken from the CPU time clock as the seed value. If you run the program more than once, each random sample will be different. The other option is to supply a seed value. In this situation, if you run the program more than once, you will obtain the same random selection each time.

For this example, the sampling method is without replacement, the sample size is 25% of the original data set, and a fixed seed is entered. If you run this task yourself and enter the same seed value (13579) as in the example, you will get the same random sample.

Using the N-Way ANOVA Task

It's time to specify your model and run the two-way ANOVA. From the Statistics task list, select N-Way ANOVA. This brings up the following:

Figure 4: Select Your Dependent Variable and Factors

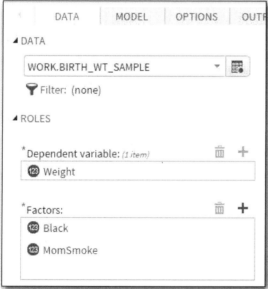

On the Data tab, select WORK.Birth_Wt_Sample (the name of your random sample), choose Weight (the weight values are in grams—1000 grams = 2.2 pounds) as the Dependent variable; choose Black (0 = not black, 1=black) and MomSmoke (0=no, 1=yes) as the factors. Select the factors in the usual way—holding down the control key and clicking your choices. See Figure 5:

Figure 5: How Factors are Selected

The next step is to click the Model tab to specify your model (Figure 6):

Figure 6: Selecting a Model

First, click Edit. This brings up the screen shown in Figure 7. Highlight the two variables Black and MomSmoke and click Full Factorial.

Figure 7: Select Black and MomSmoke in a Factorial Model

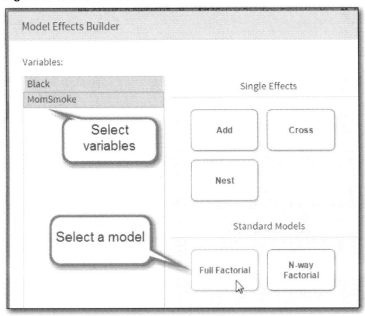

The factors in your model are then displayed on the right side of the screen (Figure 8):

Figure 8: The Task Displays Terms in Your Model

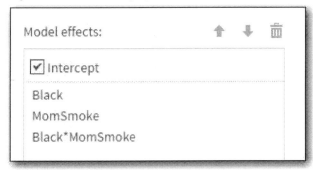

The two main effects are Black and MomSmoke, and the interaction term is shown as Black*MomSmoke.

Finally, click the Options tab to specify details for the ANOVA table and your selection of plots. In Figure 9, you see that Type 3 sums of squares is selected. Type 3 sums of squares shows the effect of each factor as if it were entered in the model last. Another way of saying this is that the analysis shows the effect of each factor after controlling for all the other factors.

Even though both main factors (Black and MomSmoke) have only two levels, you need to check the box labeled "Perform multiple comparisons" so that the program will compute the mean weights for each level of these factors.

Figure 9: Select Options

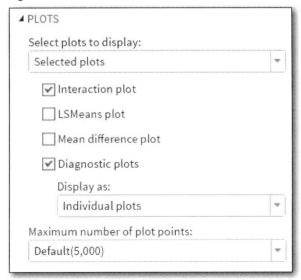

At the bottom of the Options screen, you can specify plot options (Figure 10). By choosing "Selected plots" from the plot menu, you can specify exactly what plots you want. For this example, options for an interaction plot and diagnostics plots were selected. You can choose to display the diagnostic plots as a panel (small plots all together on a single panel) or individual plots.

Figure 10: Select Plots

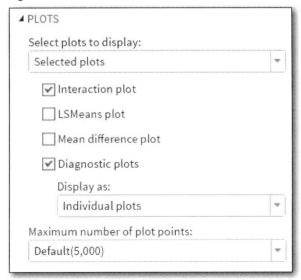

It's time to run the analysis. If you try this yourself, be aware that it can take several minutes to complete, depending on the speed of your computer and the memory allocated to your virtual computer.

You will see some output, but where are the plots? This brings up a very important lesson:

> Before examining your results, take a moment to look at the SAS log to see if there are errors or warnings.

As you can see in Figure 11, the plots were suppressed because the number of points exceeded the default value of 5,000.

Figure 11: Check the SAS Log!

```
74          proc glm data=WORK.BIRTH_WT_SAMPLE plot(only)=(diagnostics intplot);
75             class Black MomSmoke;
76             model Weight=Black MomSmoke Black*MomSmoke / ss3;
77          quit;

WARNING: ODS graphics with more than 5000 points have been suppressed. Use the PLOTS(MAXPOINTS= )
         to change or override the cutoff.
```

To fix the problem, go back to the Options tab and select No limit from the Maximum number of points to plot in the menu (Figure 12):

Figure 12: Adjust the Maximum Number of Points

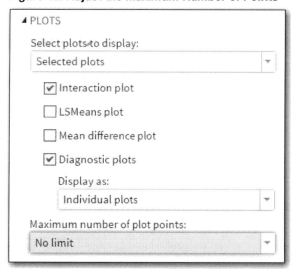

Run the program again.

The first section of the output (Figure 13) shows class-level information. As we mentioned before, it is important to verify that the number of levels and the values for these factors are what you expect. The other piece of information that is often ignored, but is very important, is the number of observations read and used. In this example, these two numbers are the same, indicating that there are no missing values for the variables selected for this analysis.

Figure 13: Class-Level Information

Class Level Information		
Class	Levels	Values
Black	2	0 1
MomSmoke	2	0 1

Number of Observations Read	12500
Number of Observations Used	12500

Next, comes the ANOVA table.

Figure 14: The ANOVA Table

Dependent Variable: Weight Infant Birth Weight

Source	DF	Sum of Squares	Mean Square	F Value	Pr > F
Model	3	201913196	67304399	224.76	<.0001
Error	12496	3741913496	299449		
Corrected Total	12499	3943826691			

R-Square	Coeff Var	Root MSE	Weight Mean
0.051197	16.22229	547.2192	3373.254

Source	DF	Type III SS	Mean Square	F Value	Pr > F
Black	1	34754959.61	34754959.61	116.06	<.0001
MomSmoke	1	43453129.92	43453129.92	145.11	<.0001
Black*MomSmoke	1	146558.23	146558.23	0.49	0.4842

At the top, are the F and p-values for the model as a whole—below, you see the sum of squares, mean squares, F and p-values for each of the two factors and the interaction term. Both of the main factors are highly significant (Black and MomSmoke) and the interaction term is not significant (at the .05 level). Of course, you first need to examine the diagnostic plots to see if the ANOVA assumptions were satisfied.

Because the program produces so many diagnostic plots, only selected ones are included here. The first plot (Figure 15) shows the residuals (the difference between each data point and the predicted mean for each combination of the factors.

Figure 15: Inspecting the Residuals

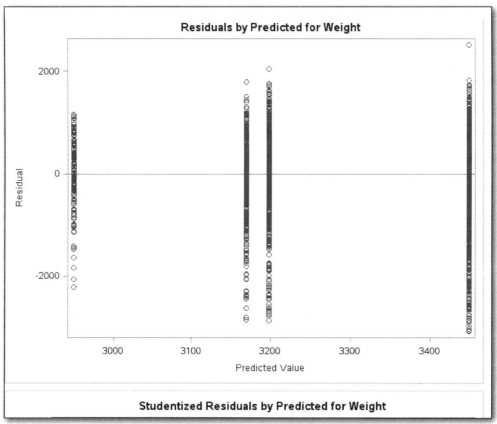

From this plot, you can see that there are a few extra outliers on the low side and that the variance is similar in each of the four categories.

Figure 16 displays a histogram of the residuals. This looks symmetric and close enough to a normal distribution to satisfy this assumption.

Figure 16: Histogram of Residuals

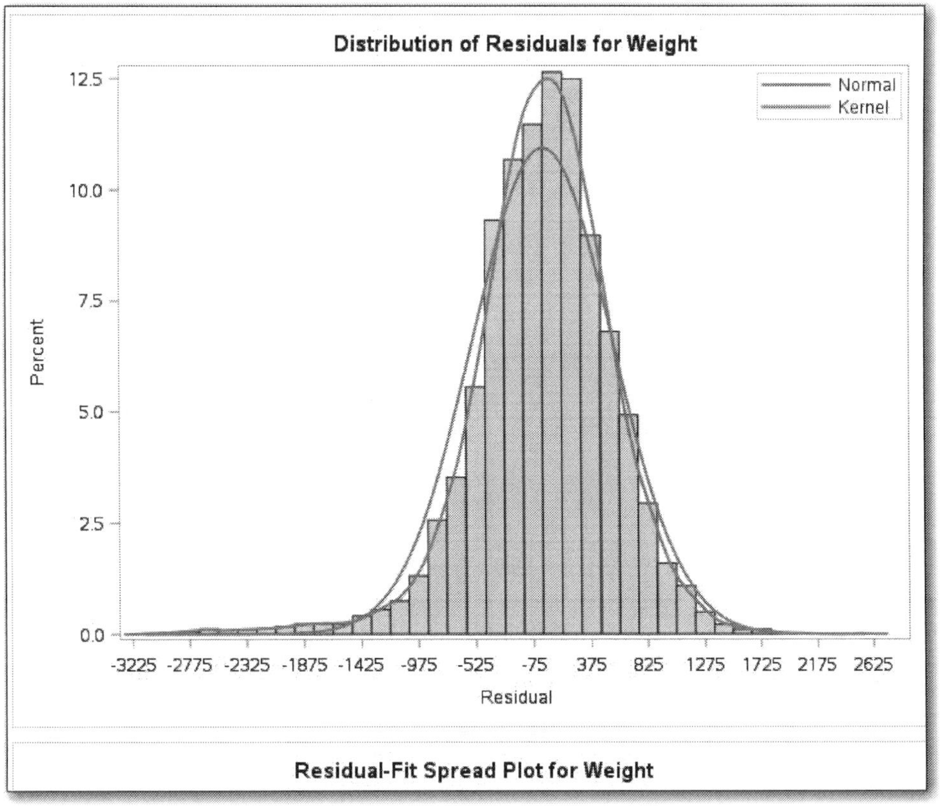

Distribution of Residuals for Weight

Residual-Fit Spread Plot for Weight

Interpreting the Two-Way ANOVA Results

Now that you are satisfied that the ANOVA assumptions were correct, let's take a moment to look at the results. Both main effects (Black and MomSmoke) were significant as shown in the ANOVA table. Because the option to produce multiple comparisons was checked on the Options tab, you obtain the following two tables:

First, you see the LSMEANS for the variable Black (Figure 17):

Figure 17: LSMEANS for Black

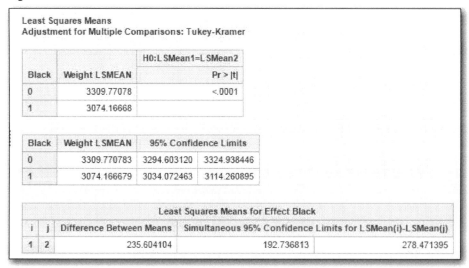

The means shown in this table are means computed from the linear model. If there are no missing values in your data set (as is the case in this data set), these means are exactly the same means that you would compute by adding up all the weights for babies born from black or non-black mothers and dividing by the number of mothers in each group, respectively. If there are missing values for any of the observations, the LSMEANS will produce a slightly different value. You see that babies born from black mothers are lighter than babies born from non-black mothers (the difference is about 236 grams (about half a pound)). The output also shows this difference along with the 95% confidence limits. Notice that these limits do not include 0, as you expect because the difference is significant at the .05 level.

The same information is displayed in Figure 18, for the variable MomSmoke.

Figure 18: LSMEANS for MomSmoke

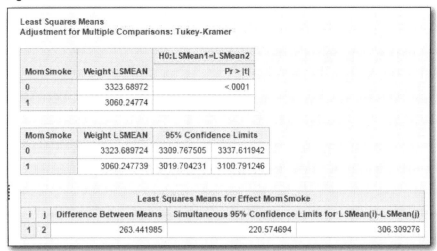

Least Squares Means
Adjustment for Multiple Comparisons: Tukey-Kramer

MomSmoke	Weight LSMEAN	H0:LSMean1=LSMean2 Pr > |t|
0	3323.68972	<.0001
1	3060.24774	

MomSmoke	Weight LSMEAN	95% Confidence Limits	
0	3323.689724	3309.767505	3337.611942
1	3060.247739	3019.704231	3100.791246

		Least Squares Means for Effect MomSmoke	
i	j	Difference Between Means	Simultaneous 95% Confidence Limits for LSMean(i)-LSMean(j)
1	2	263.441985	220.574694 306.309276

Babies born to mothers who smoke are approximately 263 grams (about half a pound) lighter than babies born to mothers who do not smoke.

Interpreting Models with Significant Interactions

It is important to inspect the interaction term before you interpret main effects in a factorial model. You can use the same data set (Birth_Wt_Sample) used in the previous example to demonstrate a model with a significant interaction term.

If you run a factorial model with MomSmoke and Married as the two factors, you obtain the following:

Figure 19: Notice a Significant Interaction Term

Dependent Variable: Weight Infant Birth Weight

Source	DF	Sum of Squares	Mean Square	F Value	Pr > F
Model	3	167654386	55884795	184.93	<.0001
Error	12496	3776172306	302190		
Corrected Total	12499	3943826691			

R-Square	Coeff Var	Root MSE	Weight Mean
0.042511	16.29639	549.7196	3373.254

Source	DF	Type III SS	Mean Square	F Value	Pr > F
MomSmoke	1	67739620.58	67739620.58	224.16	<.0001
Married	1	20004153.29	20004153.29	66.20	<.0001
MomSmoke*Married	1	4535264.42	4535264.42	15.01	0.0001

You see significant effects for the two factors as well as the interaction term. Because this analysis was run with the option to produce multiple comparisons, you can see the means for each combination of the two factors (Figure 20).

Figure 20: Adjusted Cell Means

MomSmoke	Married	Weight LSMEAN	95% Confidence Limits	
0	0	3276.341385	3256.032254	3296.650517
0	1	3454.284594	3442.264425	3466.304764
1	0	3111.914216	3074.193018	3149.635413
1	1	3175.062425	3137.728122	3212.396728

It is easier to see this graphically (see Figure 21):

Figure 21: Interaction Plot

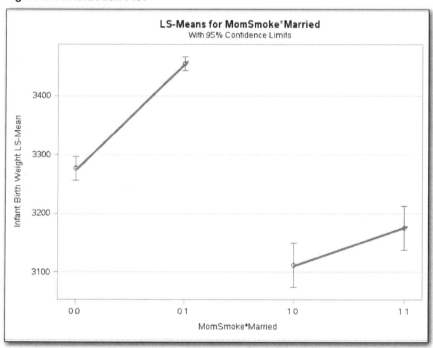

(Note: The lines between the pairs of means on this plot were added by the author; they are not included in the output.) On the x-axis, you see each combination of the two factors. The highest birth weights are found for babies whose moms do not smoke and who are married; the lowest birth weights are found for babies whose moms smoke and who are not married. However, the effect of smoking or not smoking is different for married versus unmarried moms. If there were no interactions between these factors, the two lines on the plot would be parallel. The different slopes of the two lines (and the significant p-value for the interaction term) indicate that the two factors interact with each other.

Conclusions

This chapter has demonstrated simple two-way models. Much more complex models with nested and/or crossed factors can be analyzed with the N-Way ANOVA task. Analysis of the birth weight data used in this chapter may be more meaningful by regression techniques or, if the birth weights were grouped, logistic regression. Those topics are discussed in later chapters of this book. One other thing: If you are pregnant, don't smoke!

Problems

9-1: Using the Blood_Pressure.xlsx workbook, create a temporary SAS data set (call it BP). Run a two-way ANOVA model with DBP as the dependent variable with Drug and Gender as factors. Run a full factorial model. Be sure to check the interaction term before interpreting the main effects. Include diagnostic plots in your output. Using the Tukey method, determine which Drug groups are different (if there are any).

9-2: Using the SASHELP data set HEART, run a two-way ANOVA using Weight as the dependent variable and Sex and Chol_Status (cholesterol status) as factors. Request multiple comparisons for main effects and Type 3 sum of squares only. Suppress all plots. What comparisons, if any, are significant for Chol_Status?

9-3: Using the workbook Diabetes.xls, create a temporary SAS data set (call it Diabetes) and perform a two-way ANOVA with Glucose as the dependent variable and Insulin and Diet_Drinks as factors (independent) variables. Be sure to check whether the interaction term is significant before exploring the main effects. Request multiple comparison for all effects as well as an interaction plot.

9-4: Rerun problem 9-3 except use a filter to omit the group Diet_Drinks = 'Sometimes'. Your filter statement should be:

```
Diet_Drinks ne 'Sometimes'
```

Examine the Tukey multiple comparisons for all significant factors.

9-5: You have measured the left ventricular ejection fraction (LVEF) on three groups of subjects with congestive heart failure (CHF). LVEF is the percent that the left ventricle contracts compared to a normal heart. The three groups represent 1) Placebo, 2) Calcium channel blocker, and 3) Lasix. In addition, each subject is in a normal weight group or an overweight group. The experiment resulted in the following:

```
Group      Weight      Data values for LVEF
-----------------------------------------
Placebo    Overweight  55 57 57 40 52
Placebo    Norm:       58 80 55 48 62
Calcium    Overweight  57 78 84 72 78
Calcium    Normal      65 80 81 57 55
Lasix      Overweight  60 65 48 64 40
Lasix      Normal      70 62 60 57 67
```

Run the SAS program below to create the CHF data set. The variables in this data set are Subj, Group (Placebo, Calcium, or Lasix), Weight, and LVEF.

```
data CHF;
   do Group = 'Placebo','Calcium','Lasix';
      do Weight = 'Overweight','Normal';
         do Subj = 1 to 5;
            input LVEF @@;
            output;
         end;
      end;
   end;
datalines;
55 57 57 40 52
58 80 55 48 62
57 78 84 72 78
65 80 81 57 55
60 65 48 64 40
70 62 60 57 67
;
```

You can see an explanation of how this program works from problem 8-6. The only difference is the addition of one more DO loop that creates the weight group variable.

Run a two-way ANOVA testing each of the main effects: Group and Weight.

Chapter 10: Correlation

Introduction

There are several ways to quantify the relationship between two continuous variables, the most common being a Pearson correlation coefficient. This chapter describes this as well as a nonparametric alternative called a Spearman rank-order correlation.

In addition to showing you how to compute these two correlation coefficients, you will also see how to save a SAS data set in a permanent library. Until now, all the SAS data sets created using the Import Utility or by reading raw data were stored in the Work library. Data sets in the Work library are deleted each time you close your SAS session. This is fine for homework problems or learning how to write SAS programs, but if you are working on a project that may take days (or months or years), you will want to save your SAS data sets in a permanent location.

Creating a Permanent SAS Data Set

If you plan to use only temporary SAS data sets in the WORK library, you can skim over this section or skip it entirely. Creating permanent SAS data sets in a virtual environment is somewhat more complicated than creating SAS data sets in a non-virtual environment.

One of the data sources that you are going to use to see how the correlation tasks work, is an Excel workbook called Exercise.xls, stored in c:\SASUniversityEdition\myfolders. Figure 1 shows the first few rows of this worksheet:

Figure 1: Workbook Exercise.xls

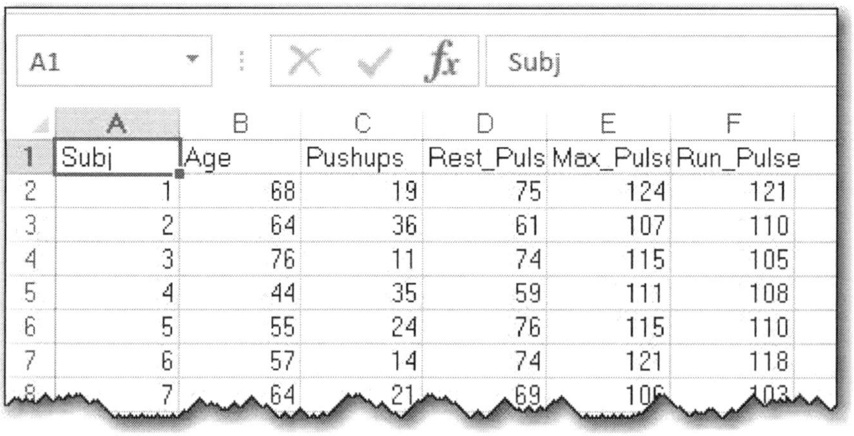

A1 | Subj

	A	B	C	D	E	F
1	Subj	Age	Pushups	Rest_Puls	Max_Puls	Run_Pulse
2	1	68	19	75	124	121
3	2	64	36	61	107	110
4	3	76	11	74	115	105
5	4	44	35	59	111	108
6	5	55	24	76	115	110
7	6	57	14	74	121	118
8	7	64	21	69	[illegible]	[illegible]

This worksheet contains information on age, the number of pushups a person can perform, and pulse rates under three conditions: resting, maximal exertion, and while running. By the way, the data values are not real—they was generated by a small SAS program that used random number generators in such a way that certain variables would be related to others.

There are 50 subjects in the file. Notice that the column headings are all valid SAS variable names. The first step is to use the Import Utility to convert this workbook into a SAS data set.

Because you want this data set to be permanent, you need to create what is called a SAS library. You have already seen the SASHELP and WORK libraries. For this exercise you are going to create a new library called BOOKDATA.

SAS library names (also called librefs—library references) are created with a LIBNAME statement. Library names are a maximum of eight characters in length and follow the same naming conventions as SAS variable names and SAS data sets. That is, they must begin with a letter or underscore with the remaining characters being letters, digits, or the underscore character.

Rather than having to write a LIBNAME statement, you will see how SAS Studio can create this statement for you and save it in a location called AUTOEXEC.SAS. The advantage of saving the LIBNAME statement there is that the library will be available every time you open a SAS session. This is important because SAS libraries must be created every time you open a new session.

To have SAS Studio do all this work for you, first click Server Files and Folders and place the cursor on the shared folder Book_Data (see Figure 2): To review how this shared folder was created, refer to the shared folders section in Chapter 3.

Figure 2: The Shared Folder Created in VirtualBox

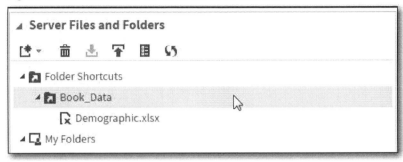

Now, right-click on this folder shortcut, select Create and then click Library (Figure 3):

Figure 3: Creating a Permanent Library

Be sure to check the box to re-create this library at start-up (Figure 4):

Figure 4: Creating the New Library

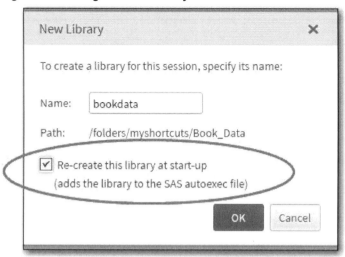

Clicking OK adds the appropriate LIBNAME statement that is written to AUTOEXEC.SAS. Here is a screen shot of AUTOEXEC.SAS, with the new LIBNAME statement outlined:

Figure 5: AUTOEXEC.SAS with New LIBNAME Statement Added

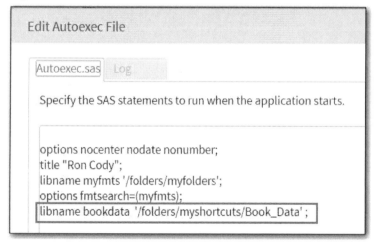

Now, every time you start a SAS session, the BOOKDATA library will be available for you to read or write SAS data sets.

One final note: The actual folder on your hard drive is c:\book\Book_Data (it contains an underscore character). This is the same name that you gave to the shared folder that you created using Oracle VirtualBox. It is important to remember that the name of the shared folder cannot contain any blanks. The library name that identifies this folder (BOOKDATA) does not contain the underscore character. Why? Although an underscore character is valid in a library name, adding it would exceed the 8-character maximum length for library names. As a matter of fact, the name that you choose for this library name does not need to have any relationship to the actual folder name. It just makes sense to use a name that helps you remember the actual folder name. The good news is that once you have checked the option to create the library name at start-up using the Autoexec file, you can always check this file to see what library name you used and the name of the shared folder. Now you see why placing your data files and SAS data sets in SASUniversityEdition\myfolders is a good idea.

Reading the Exercise.xls Workbook and Creating a Permanent SAS Data Set

To convert the Exercise.xls workbook into a permanent SAS data set, proceed as you did with all the previous Excel workbook examples in this book:

Tasks and Utilities ▶ Utilities ▶ Import Data

This time, when you change the name of the output data set, select the BOOKDATA library and call the data set Exercise (see Figure 6):

Figure 6: Saving the Exercise Data Set in the BOOKDATA Library

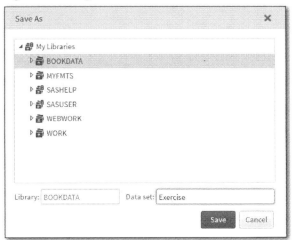

When you look in Server Files and Folders, you will see a file called exercise.sas7bdat listed under the folder shortcut Book_Data. SAS uses the extension sas7bdat for its data set names (see Figure 7):

Figure 7: The SAS Data Set Is Listed under Folder Shortcuts - Book_Data

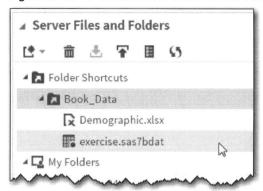

Using the Statistics Correlation Task

As a quick summary, a Person correlation coefficient measures the strength of the relationship between two variables. These variables are usually continuous, but there are types of correlations where one or both of the values are binary (0 or 1) or ordinal variables. The formula for calculating Pearson correlation coefficients (from here on, just called correlations) is such that correlation values lie between -1 and +1, inclusive. Positive correlations indicate a positive relationship between two variables. For example, height and weight would be correlated for a group of young children. The taller children would tend to be heavier and vice versa. Correlations near zero tell you that given a value for one of the variables, you have no better guess for the value of the other variable. Finally, correlations near -1 indicate a strong inverse relationship between two values; as one increases, the other decreases. For example, the dose of insulin would be negatively correlated with blood sugar levels—the higher the dose, the lower the blood sugar level.

It is important to remember two things about correlations. First, it doesn't matter which variable you place on the x- or y-axis. Second, the correlation is strongly influenced by outliers. The following two figures show the effect of a single outlier on a set of data points that, without the outlier, has a correlation close to zero.

First, here is a scatter plot of x-y data with a correlation close to zero:

Figure 8: X and Y with Close to a Zero Correlation

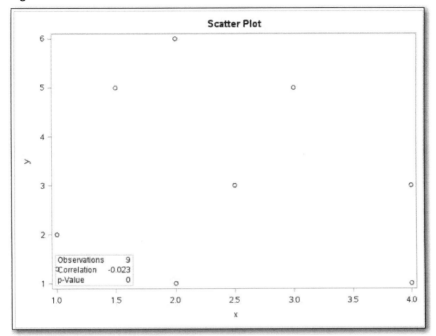

The correlation is -0.023 (almost zero). Here is the same set of Xs and Ys with a single outlier (x=11, y=12) added:

Figure 9: Sample Plot with a Single Outlier

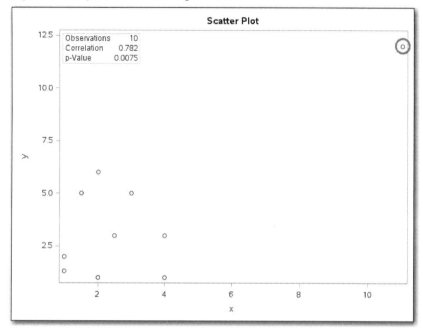

The correlation is now .782. .The lesson here is that outliers can have a very large effect on Pearson correlation coefficients. In looking at extreme outliers, you might want to do two things: one is to make sure it isn't a data entry error, and the second is to make sure that this case is really appropriately considered to be part of the population under consideration. For example, if you were looking at the relationship between income and school achievement, and one of your sample was a multi-billionaire, you might want to remove that data point from the sample. Of course, in doing so, you would want to say that you had done that in any article or report you wrote concerning those data.

This brings up one of the most important rules about reporting correlation coefficients in a study: Always inspect a scatter plot to identify data points that may have undue influence.

It's time to investigate correlations among the variables in the Exercise data set. Start by clicking on Tasks and Utilities. Then choose Statistics, and finally, Correlation Analysis:

Tasks and Utilities ▶ Statistics ▶ Correlation Analysis

Generating Correlation and Scatter Plot Matrices

The Correlation DATA tab looks like this:

Figure 10: The Correlation DATA Tab

You have a choice. One is to enter all the numeric variables of interest in the Analysis variables box (as was done here) to compute correlations between every pair of variables. As an alternative, select one or more variables in the Analysis box and other variables in the Correlate with box. If you do this, the task will compute correlations for every combination of the Analysis variables and the Correlate with variables. For example, if you have variables A and B in the Analysis variables box and variables X, Y, and Z in the Correlate with box, the task will compute the correlations for the pairs: AX, AY, AZ, BX, BY, and BZ.

Looking at the Options tab (Figure 11 below), you have chosen to generate a matrix of scatter plots and you have checked the option to include histograms on the diagonal of the matrix.

Figure 11: Correlation Analysis OPTIONS Tab

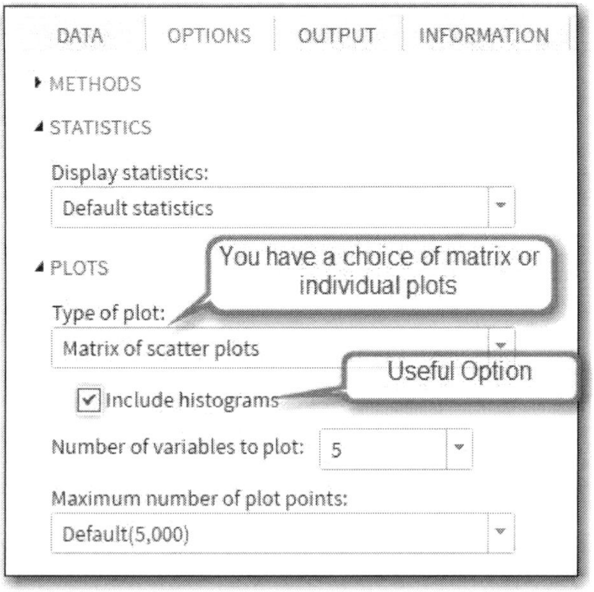

Figure 12 shows the correlation matrix:

Figure 12: Correlation Matrix

5 Variables:	Age Pushups Rest_Pulse Max_Pulse Run_Pulse

Pearson Correlation Coefficients, N = 50 Prob > |r| under H0: Rho=0					
	Age	**Pushups**	**Rest_Pulse**	**Max_Pulse**	**Run_Pulse**
Age Age	1.00000	-0.49191 0.0003	0.48774 0.0003	0.26582 0.0621	0.25097 0.0788
Pushups Pushups	-0.49191 0.0003	1.00000	-0.49639 0.0002	-0.45010 0.0010	-0.34555 0.0140
Rest_Pulse Rest_Pulse	0.48774 0.0003	-0.49639 0.0002	1.00000	0.83112 <.0001	0.76139 <.0001
Max_Pulse Max_Pulse	0.26582 0.0621	-0.45010 0.0010	0.83112 <.0001	1.00000	0.93634 <.0001
Run_Pulse Run_Pulse	0.25097 0.0788	-0.34555 0.0140	0.76139 <.0001	0.93634 <.0001	1.00000

The intersection of each row and column in this table shows you the correlation coefficient (top number) and the *p*-value (the bottom number). For example, the correlation between Age and Pushups is -.49191 with a *p*-value of .0003. The older the subject, the fewer pushups he or she could do. Because of the symmetry of the matrix, you only need to look at the upper or lower triangle of the matrix.

Before you spend time investigating the correlation coefficient, you should take a moment to inspect the *p*-value. What does it mean to have a "significant" correlation? To understand the *p*-value, imagine two variables that are completely unrelated—the correlation between them is 0 (see Figure 13 below):

Figure 13: Population with a Zero Correlation

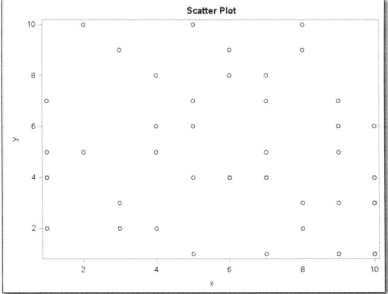

Now, imagine taking a random sample of 5 subjects from this population. You might wind up with a selection that looks like the circled points in Figure 14. The problem is that, with a small sample, you may, by chance, end up with a correlation that is either close to 1 or close to -1. The *p*-value that you see in the correlation tables is the probability that you would obtain a correlation with an absolute value as large as or larger than the one you obtained by chance alone, given that the true population correlation between your two variables is actually 0.

Figure 14: Random Sample: Correlation = .8

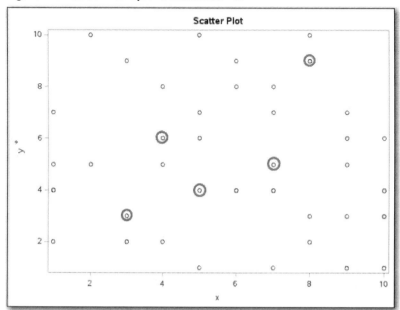

Now, back to the output. Following the correlation matrix is a matrix of scatter plots. Because you checked the box to include histograms on the diagonal, they are included as well (see Figure 15):

Figure 15: Scatter Plot Matrix

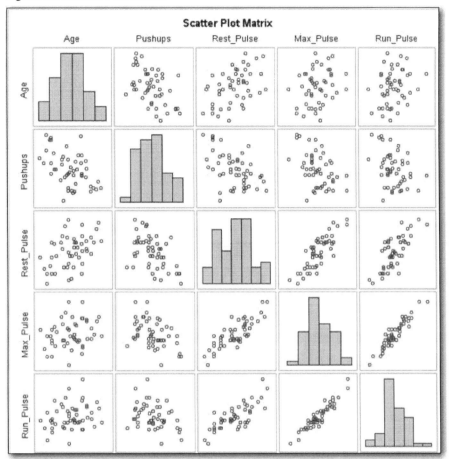

Here you see a scatter plot for all combinations of the variables (corresponding to the correlation matrix above). This scatter plot matrix is an excellent way to see relationships among the variables in your data set.

If you choose individual scatter plots instead of a scatter plot matrix, each of the small plots displayed in the matrix is displayed as an individual plot. A typical plot looks like the one displaying Max_Pulse versus Rest_Pulse in the figure below:

Figure 16: Example of an Individual Scatter Plot

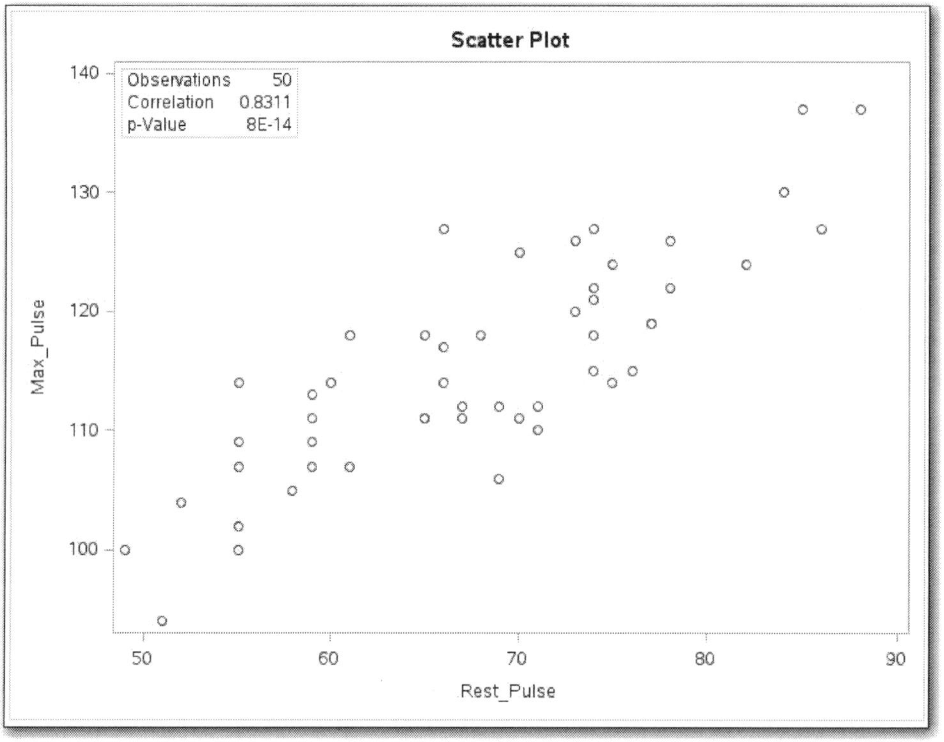

Interpreting Correlation Coefficients

The question often comes up: "What is a large correlation?" The short answer is "that depends." That's not very satisfying. A useful approach to interpreting a correlation coefficient is to square it. The value of r-square is the proportion of variance (the standard deviation squared) of one of the variables that can be explained by the other. For example, look at the correlation between Run_Pulse and Rest_Pulse. It is .76139, and this value squared is .5797. Both of these variables differ among the subjects, and you can compute the variance of each of the resting and running pulse rates. Because the value of r-square is .5797, you can say that 57.97% of the variance in the running pulse rate can be explained by the fact that these subjects all have different resting pulse rates.

Generating Spearman Non-Parametric Correlations

As with many statistical tests, there is a nonparametric alternative to a Pearson correlation. One of the most popular is called a Spearman correlation. The Spearman method substitutes ranks for the two variables and then computes a correlation on the ranks. When there are outliers on your scatter plot, you may want to consider computing Spearman correlations. As a matter of fact, it's not a bad idea to routinely compute both Pearson and Spearman correlations and take special notice when they produce substantially different results.

To add Spearman correlations to the output of the Correlation analysis tab, expand the Nonparametric tab and click the box next to Spearman's rank-order correlation (see Figure 17):

Figure 17: Requesting Spearman Correlations

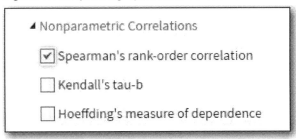

Two variables, Run_Pulse and Rest_Pulse, were selected for this example. The resulting output is shown below:

Figure 18: Pearson and Spearman Correlations

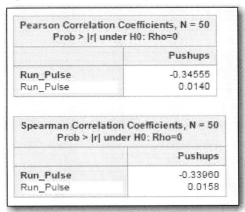

The value of the Spearman correlation (-.33960) is almost identical to the Pearson correlation (r=-.34555). When you have outliers or other non-normal distributions, these two values may be quite different.

Conclusions

The correlation analysis statistics task enables you to correlate one set of variables with another or to produce a correlation matrix showing correlations between every pair of variables. You should routinely request either individual plots or a scatter plot matrix as part of the procedure. Finally, consider computing Spearman rank-order correlations.

Problems

10-1: Start with the Excel workbook Blood_Pressure.xlsx and create a temporary SAS data set called BP. Compute a Pearson and Spearman (nonparametric) correlation between the two variables SBP and DBP. Select the appropriate option to print a scatter plot.

10-2: Using the SASHELP data set Heart, compute a correlation matrix with the variables Height, Weight, and Cholesterol. Be sure to include p-values in the table. Request a matrix of scatter plots and be sure to set the number of points plotted to unlimited.

10-3: Take a random sample of size 500 from the SASHELP.Heart data set (use a fixed seed of 13579). Call the sample Sample_Heart. Include all the variables in the sample. Repeat problem 10-2 using the random sample. Compare the correlations and p-values between the full data set and the sample.

10-4: Run the program below to create a SAS data set called Corr_Population. Run the Correlation Analysis task to confirm that the correlation between X and Y is close to zero. Next, use the Select Random Sample task under Data tasks to create a random sample of seven from Corr_Population. Compute the correlation between X and Y in this random sample. Do this several times (you can just click on the two tabs for Select Random Sample and Correlation Analysis) and notice how the correlation changes each time.

```
data Corr_Population;
    call streaminit(12345);
    do i = 1 to 1000;
        X = ceil(rand('uniform')*100);
        Y = ceil(rand('uniform')*100);
        output;
    end;
    drop i;
run;
```

For the reader who is interested in this SAS program, the RAND function with the argument 'uniform' produces uniform random numbers between 0 and 1. The call routine CALL STREAMINIT enables you to select a fixed seed value to initiate the random sequence. The statements that compute the X and Y values produce random integers from 1 to 100. Because both X and Y are randomly determined, the correlation between them should (and is) close to zero. You can use the List Data task or PROC PRINT to print the first few observations in this data set.

10-5: Use the DATA step below to create a data set called Outlier.

```
data Outlier;
    input X Y @@;
datalines;
0 2 5 6 6 2 3 3 1 3 4 4 8 1 6 4 2 5 4 2 6 5
;
```

Compute the correlation between X and Y. Then add the single data point x=15, Y=15, and rerun the correlation task. Request both a Pearson and Spearman correlation. What lesson is to be learned from this problem? Note: To add the additional data point, place two 15s separated by spaces at the end of the line of data in the program.

Chapter 11: Simple and Multiple Regression

Introduction

Correlation analysis identifies relationships between variables—regression analysis allows you to predict one variable based on values of another variable (simple regression) or a combination of variables (multiple regression).

The concept behind simple or multiple regression is to select one or more variables (sometimes called predictor variables) that can be combined to predict an outcome (dependent variable). The models described in this book are all linear models.

There are several reasons why regression techniques are useful. One reason is that we can use the resulting regression equation to predict a value. For example, given the gender, height, and weight of a person, you could predict the maximum lung volume for that person. Another reason why regression is used is to help explain the relation among a set of variables. That is, we can look at the influence of one or more variables to better understand the nature of a dependent variable. If more than one predictor variable is used, the analysis looks at all predictor variables simultaneously.

Regression, especially multiple regression, needs to be done carefully. There are a number of diagnostic plots produced by the regression task that are useful in deciding if the assumptions for regression are met by your data. In addition, you can test for influential data points (data values that can change the results of the analysis if they are included or not), and test for multi-collinearity (predictor variables correlated with each other). Including highly correlated predictor variables in a multiple regression can lead to strange and paradoxical results.

Describing Simple Linear Regression

Let's use the permanent SAS data set Exercise, described in the last chapter to demonstrate simple (that is, single predictor variable) linear regression. Intuition (plus the correlation matrix produced in the last chapter) tells you that there should be a positive relationship between a person's resting heart rate and this person's pulse rate while running. To run a regression on these two variables, call up the Linear regression task:

Tasks and Utilities ▶ Statistics ▶ Linear regression

It looks like this:

Figure 1: Select Data Source and Specify Variables

You see that the Exercise data set, located in the BOOKDATA library is selected in the Data field; Run_Pulse is selected as the dependent variable and Rest_Pulse is selected as a continuous (independent) variable.

The next step is to specify your model. Click the Model tab to do this:

Figure 2: Specify the Model

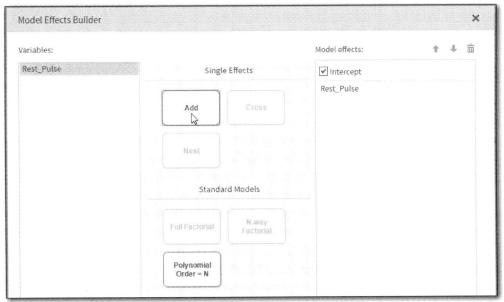

First, click Edit and then highlight Rest_Pulse in the Variables list. Next, click Add to add this variable to the model. In the box labeled Model effects, you now see the intercept and Rest_Pulse listed. Click OK to continue.

The last step, before running the model, is to click Options. This tab allows you to select additional statistics and plots:

Figure 3: Specify Plots

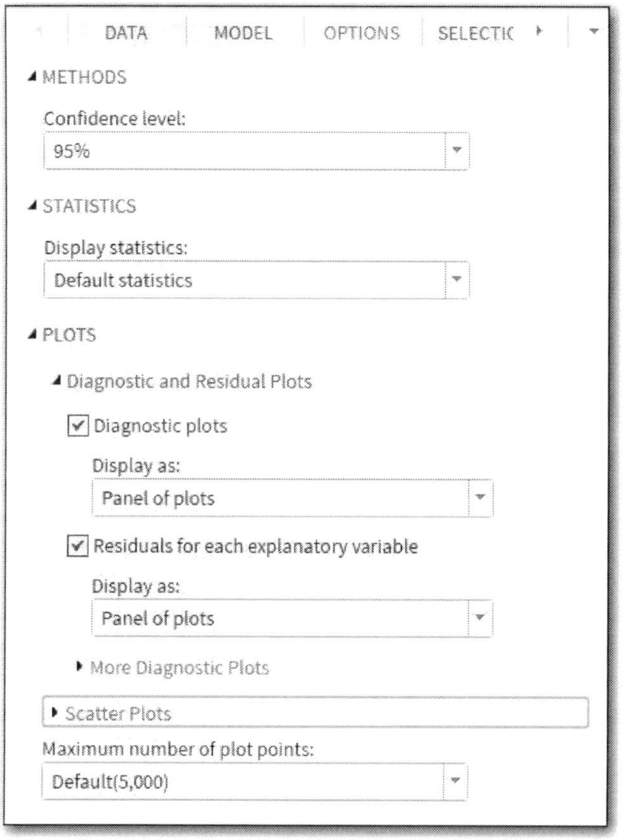

Select Diagnostic plots and Residuals for each explanatory variable. You can request the residual plots as a panel of plots or individual plots. For most situations, a panel of plots is sufficient. (Note: The diagnostic plots shown in this chapter are actually selected from individual plots.)

It's time to run the model. The first section of output is the ANOVA table shown in Figure 4:

Figure 4: Regression Results

Model: MODEL1
Dependent Variable: Run_Pulse Run_Pulse

Number of Observations Read	50
Number of Observations Used	50

		Analysis of Variance			
Source	DF	Sum of Squares	Mean Square	F Value	Pr > F
Model	1	2484.46062	2484.46062	66.21	<.0001
Error	48	1801.21938	37.52540		
Corrected Total	49	4285.68000			

Root MSE	6.12580	R-Square	0.5797
Dependent Mean	112.92000	Adj R-Sq	0.5710
Coeff Var	5.42490		

Because the number of observations read and used are equal (with a value of 50), you know that there were no missing values for the variables Rest_Pulse and Run_Pulse. The mean square due to the model is much larger than the mean square due to error, yielding a very large F-value and a low *p*-value. The mean of the dependent variable (Run_Pulse) is 112.92, and the R-square is .5710. The linear regression task also computes an adjusted R-square. This value is useful when you have several independent variables in the model. The addition of independent variables in a model causes the value of R-square to increase even if independent variables are only randomly correlated with the dependent variable. The value labeled Adj R-Sq adjusts for the number of independent variables in your model and is a way to compare models with different numbers of independent variables.

The next section of the output (Figure 5) shows the intercept and slope of the regression line:

Figure 5: Parameter Estimates

	Parameter Estimates					
Variable	Label	DF	Parameter Estimate	Standard Error	t Value	Pr > |t|
Intercept	Intercept	1	63.15163	6.17751	10.22	<.0001
Rest_Pulse	Rest_Pulse	1	0.73297	0.09008	8.14	<.0001

You are not interested in the value of the intercept, except in estimating value of Run_Pulse. (The intercept would be the value of Run_Pulse for a Rest_Pulse of 0, a condition requiring immediate medical attention.) The parameter estimate for Rest_Pulse (.73297) is the slope of the regression line. To compute a value of Run_Pulse for any given value of Rest_Pulse, use this equation:

```
Run_Pulse = 63.15163 + .73297*Rest_Pulse
```

Figure 6 shows the actual data points, the regression line, and two types of confidence limits.

Figure 6: Regression Line, Confidence Limits, and Sources of Variation

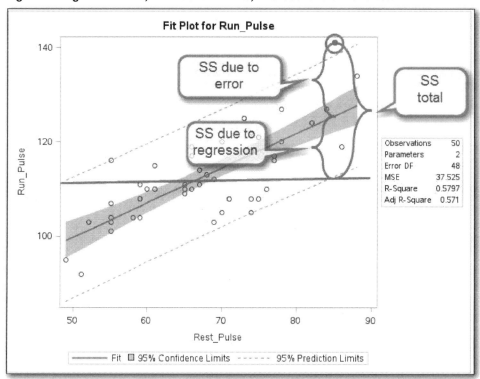

To help explain the two sources of variation in a simple linear model, a single data point was selected (located in the upper-right side of the plot). The horizontal line on the plot is the mean of Run_Pulse for the total sample (it is 112.92). The selected data point contributes to the total sum of squares for two reasons. First, given a value of Rest_Pulse equal to about 85 (the value of Rest_Pulse for the selected point), you would expect a Run_Pulse value of about 125 (the value that lies on the regression line). The difference between the mean Run_Pulse and the point on the regression line represents the amount that the regression contributes to the sum of squares for this particular point. The difference between the regression line and each data point (called a residual) contributes to the error sum of squares. If all the data points were close to the regression line, most of the contributions to the sum of squares would be due to the regression, and a smaller portion would be due to error, indicating a good fit.

The shaded portion of this graph represents the 95% confidence limit for the prediction of Run_Pulse for any given value of Rest_Pulse. The other, much wider confidence limits are for individual data points. Given a value of Rest_Pulse, you are 95% confident that a random data point will be within these limits.

Understanding the Diagnostic Plots

Before you start interpreting the relatively high R-square and the low *p*-value for this model, you need to look at some diagnostic plots to determine if the residuals are normally distributed and if the variance of the residuals seems homogeneous across different values of Rest_Pulse. These are two assumptions behind linear regression. It's time to inspect some of the diagnostic plots:

Figure 7 is one of the diagnostic plots produced by the regression task. It shows the difference between the actual value of Run_Pulse and the value predicted by the regression.

Figure 7: Residual Plot

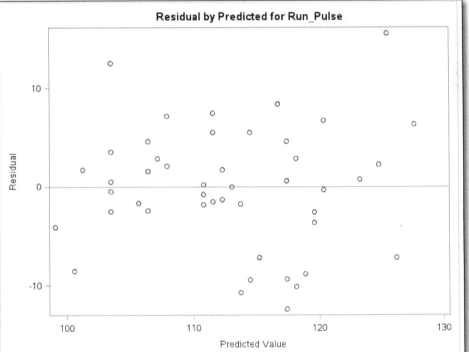

There are several things to notice in this plot. First, the points seem mostly random. If you saw a pattern in these points (such as the points curving up or down), you might suspect that a non-linear component could improve the model. Next, the spread of the points around 0 does not tend to increase or decrease with different values of Run_Pulse. To inspect the distribution of the residuals, you can inspect the Q-Q plot (Figure 8), included as one of the diagnostic plots.

Figure 8: Q-Q Plot of the Residuals

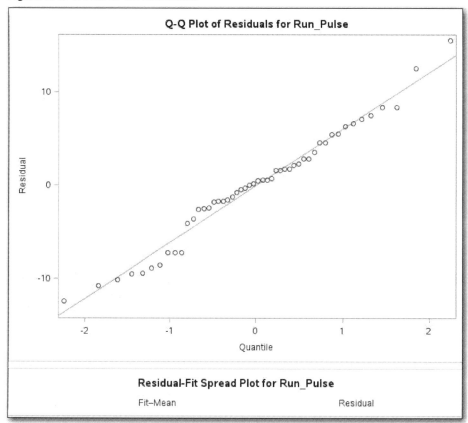

Notice that the points on this plot fall very closely around the straight line. This demonstrates that the assumption that the residuals are normally distributed is satisfied.

The last plot that is discussed here shows Cook's D for values of Run_Pulse.

Figure 9: Cook's D for Run_Pulse

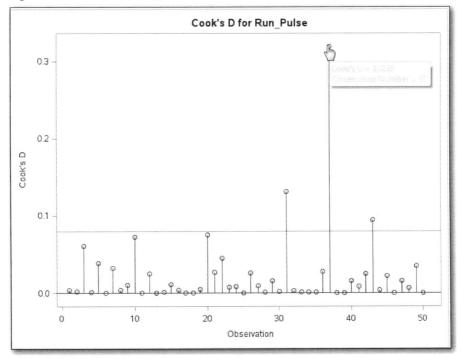

Cook's D is a measure of influence for each data point. There are several measures of influence available in the regression task. They all involve running the regression with and without each data point removed to see if the removal of a particular data point changes either the predicted value or the betas (coefficients) in the regression equation. Cook's D measures changes in the predicted value when a data point is removed. Large values for Cook's D indicate these points are influential. If you place your cursor on one of these large values (see the hand pointer on the plot) the ID for that data point is displayed. You may want to check that this data point is a valid data point and not the result of a data error.

Demonstrating Multiple Regression

Multiple regression, as the name implies, uses more than one predictor variable to estimate a single dependent variable. You can use the same Exercise data set used in the simple linear regression section to see how to run a multiple regression using SAS Studio. A useful first step is to use the Correlation task to produce a correlation matrix for all the variables of interest. The next two figures are screen shots of the correlation matrix and the scatter plot matrix when the variables Age, Pushups, Rest_Pulse, Run_Pulse, and Max_Pulse are entered as analysis variables.

To obtain the scatter plot matrix, the Plot option was selected, and the box labeled "Include histograms" was checked. Here are the results:

Figure 10: Correlation Matrix for the Exercise Data Set

				Pearson Correlation Coefficients, N = 50 Prob > |r| under H0: Rho=0					
	Age	Pushups	Rest_Pulse	Max_Pulse	Run_Pulse
Age Age	1.00000	-0.49191 0.0003	0.48774 0.0003	0.26582 0.0621	0.25097 0.0788
Pushups Pushups	-0.49191 0.0003	1.00000	-0.49639 0.0002	-0.45010 0.0010	-0.34555 0.0140
Rest_Pulse Rest_Pulse	0.48774 0.0003	-0.49639 0.0002	1.00000	0.83112 <.0001	0.76139 <.0001
Max_Pulse Max_Pulse	0.26582 0.0621	-0.45010 0.0010	0.83112 <.0001	1.00000	0.93634 <.0001
Run_Pulse Run_Pulse	0.25097 0.0788	-0.34555 0.0140	0.76139 <.0001	0.93634 <.0001	1.00000

Figure 11: Scatter Plot Matrix for the Exercise Data Set

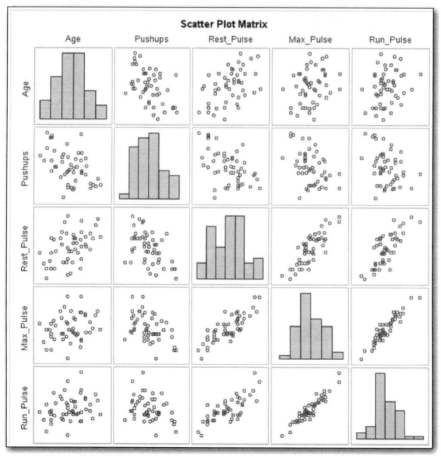

It is clear from both figures that there are some strong correlations among the variables. The condition where the predictor variables are highly correlated is called multi-collinearity, and it causes serious problems when these variables are all used in multiple regression (as you will see).

So, going on with the demonstration, let's use the variables Age, Pushups, Rest_Pulse, and Max_Pulse to predict Run_Pulse. Select the Linear Regression task; select the BOOKDATA.Exercise data set; and choose Run_Pulse for the dependent variable and all the predictor variables in the box labeled Continuous variables. On the Model tab, select all the variables, click Add, and then click OK.

When you run the task, here is what you will see:

Figure 12: ANOVA Table for Multiple Regression

Analysis of Variance					
Source	DF	Sum of Squares	Mean Square	F Value	Pr > F
Model	4	3800.80979	950.20245	88.19	<.0001
Error	45	484.87021	10.77489		
Corrected Total	49	4285.68000			

Root MSE	3.28251	R-Square	0.8869	
Dependent Mean	112.92000	Adj R-Sq	0.8768	
Coeff Var	2.90694			

Notice that the model is highly significant, and the R-square (.8869) and the adjusted R-square (.8768) are fairly large. However, take a look at the parameter estimates (Figure 13):

Figure 13: Parameter Estimates for the Multiple Regression

Parameter Estimates						
Variable	Label	DF	Parameter Estimate	Standard Error	t Value	Pr > |t|
Intercept	Intercept	1	-7.80929	8.04006	-0.97	0.3366
Age	Age	1	0.03955	0.03738	1.06	0.2956
Pushups	Pushups	1	0.08573	0.04576	1.87	0.0675
Rest_Pulse	Rest_Pulse	1	-0.06462	0.10016	-0.65	0.5221
Max_Pulse	Max_Pulse	1	1.04744	0.09786	10.70	<.0001

In the earlier simple regression model, Rest_Pulse was highly significant in predicting Run_Pulse ($p < .0001$), and the slope (labeled parameter estimate) was positive—here Rest_Pulse is not significant ($p = .5221$), and the parameter estimate is negative. What's going on?

This result is typical in cases where you have highly correlated predictor variables. You already knew this was the case when you saw the correlation matrix of the variables. This phenomenon is called multi-collinearity. One popular diagnostic test for multi-collinearity is call the VIF. This stands for variance inflation factor. Here's how it works:

If you take each of the predictor variables one at a time and perform a multiple regression with the selected predictor variable as the dependent variable and the remaining predictor variables as independent variables, you will get an R-square for each predictor variable. High values of R-square indicate that a particular predictor variable is correlated with a linear combination of the other predictor variables. Think of it as the degree to which the variable under consideration is more or less already accounted for by the other variables in the regression. Rather than use the R-square values, the VIF is computed as follows:

$$VIF_i = \frac{1}{(1 - R_i^2)}$$

For example, if an R-square was equal to .9, the VIF would be 1/(1-.9) = 10. Therefore, large values of VIF indicate multi-collinearity problems.

To include the VIF in your regression, click the Options tab, expand the menu next to Display statistics, and select Collinearity. Check the box for Variance inflation factors (Figure 14):

Figure 14: Option for Variance Inflation Factor (VIF)

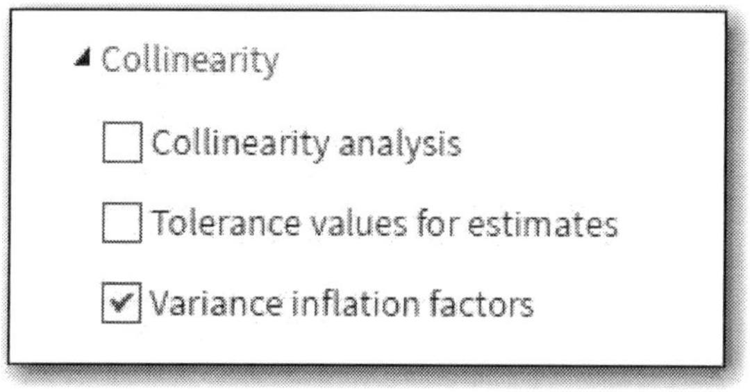

With this option checked, the parameter estimates table includes the value of the VIF for each predictor variable. Here is the result:

Figure 15; Parameter Estimates with VIF Added

			Parameter	Standard			Variance
Variable	Label	DF	Estimate	Error	t Value	Pr > |t|	Inflation
Intercept	Intercept	1	-7.80929	8.04006	-0.97	0.3366	0
Age	Age	1	0.03955	0.03738	1.06	0.2956	1.65524
Pushups	Pushups	1	0.08573	0.04576	1.87	0.0675	1.54495
Rest_Pulse	Rest_Pulse	1	-0.06462	0.10016	-0.65	0.5221	4.30537
Max_Pulse	Max_Pulse	1	1.04744	0.09786	10.70	<.0001	3.65824

The largest value of VIF is found for Rest_Pulse. The decision of which variables to remove from the regression can be determined by choosing the variables with the highest *p*-values or highest VIF values. Typically, you take out one variable at a time, rerun the model, and check the VIFs. For this example, Rest_Pulse was removed and the model rerun. See Figure 16:

Figure 16: Model with the Least Significant Variable (Rest_Pulse) Removed

			Parameter Estimates				
Variable	Label	DF	Parameter Estimate	Standard Error	t Value	Pr > |t|	Variance Inflation
Intercept	Intercept	1	-5.76862	7.34483	-0.79	0.4362	0
Age	Age	1	0.02876	0.03321	0.87	0.3910	1.32353
Pushups	Pushups	1	0.08691	0.04544	1.91	0.0620	1.54251
Max_Pulse	Max_Pulse	1	0.99630	0.05702	17.47	<.0001	1.25817

Notice that all the VIFs are low, and the coefficient of Max_Pulse is positive (as it should be). This section should encourage you to check the VIF and inspect a correlation matrix each time you conduct a multiple regression.

This example is a fairly extreme one in that one of the predictor variables has an unusually high simple correlation with the outcome variable, and the independent (predictor) variables tend to be intercorrelated substantially as well. What has been presented here is a purely data-based approach to working with this situation. But in real life, you will almost always want to bring your understanding of the nature of the variables into consideration in analyzing the data. For example, Age is a very different kind of variable from Max_Pulse. And Max_Pulse may be conceptually very close to Run_Pulse. The question of "Just what do I want to explain here?" has to be taken into consideration. But that is a long discussion, and not really the goal of this book. In general, using more than three independent variables, especially ones with a fair amount of intercorrelation, will almost always lead to difficulties in interpretation.

Demonstrating Stepwise Multiple Regression

The final section in this chapter describes several automatic methods for selecting predictor variables in a multiple regression model. Clicking the Selection tab brings up the following screen:

Figure 17: Selection Methods for Multiple Regression

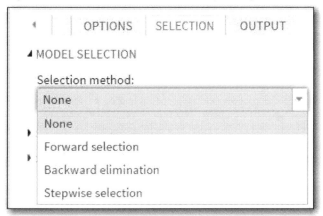

If you leave the default value of None, the regression task will enter all of the predictor variables that you have selected, either as Classification variables or Continuous variables. The other three methods in the list represent automatic selection methods.

Each of these automatic selection methods allows you to choose a criterion for entering or removing variables. The default method is called the Schwarz Bayesian Information Criterion (abbreviated SBC). This method aims to find a model with good predictive properties while limiting the number of predictor variables in the model (called a parsimonious model). Another popular selection method uses the value of R-square or the adjusted R-square to determine which variable to enter or remove from the model.

If you select forward selection as your selection method and R-square as your method to add or remove variables, the program first chooses the variable with the highest R-square value (lowest *p*-value). It continues to enter the remaining variables based on values of R-square until the *p*-value for a variable exceeds a default value.

Backward selection is just the opposite—it starts with all the variables in the model and removes them one-by-one until a criterion is met.

One of the most popular selection methods is the last one in the list—stepwise selection. This method is similar to forward selection except that variables already selected may be removed if adding other variables causes a particular variable to no longer satisfy the selection criterion. To demonstrate an automatic selection process, let's use the 25% random sample of birth weights from the SASHELP data set Bweight (first discussed in Chapter 6).

You start this task by selecting the Birth_Wt_Sample data set in the WORK library. The dependent variable is Weight. The two variables Black (1=black, 0=non-black) and MomSmoke (1=yes, 0=no) are selected as classification variables and the two variables MomAge (mother's age) and MomWtGain (mom's weight gain) are selected as continuous variables. (See Figure 18 below):

Figure 18: Choosing Classification and Continuous Variables for Multiple Regression

Click the Selection tab to choose a selection method.

Figure 19: Choosing a Selection Method

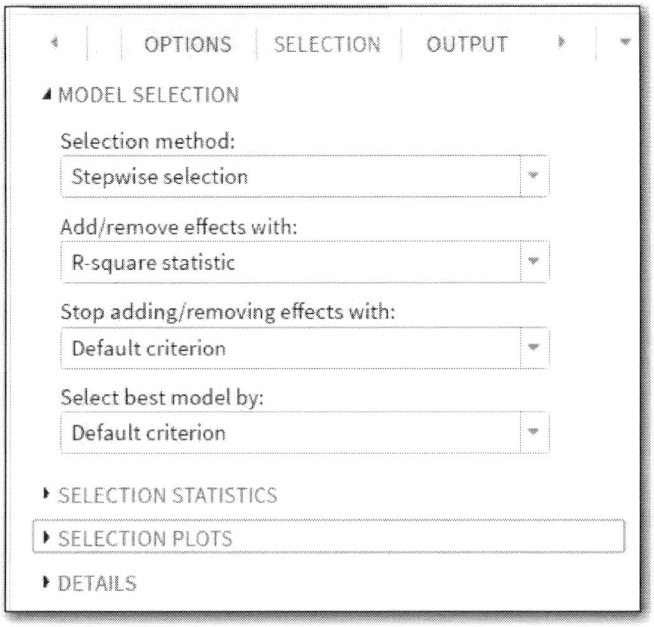

For this example, you have chosen stepwise regression and R-square as the add/remove criterion. It's time to run the model. The first section of output shows the selection method and criterion for entering or removing a variable (Figure 20):

Figure 20: Results Showing Selection Method and Select and Stopping Criterion

Data Set	WORK.BIRTH_WT_SAMPLE
Dependent Variable	Weight
Selection Method	Stepwise
Select Criterion	R-Square
Stop Criterion	R-Square
Effect Hierarchy Enforced	None

The next part of the output shows the values for all of your classification variables (Figure 21):

Figure 21: Class Level Information

Class Level Information		
Class	Levels	Values
Black	2	0 1
Mom Smoke	2	0 1

Now comes the good stuff: The stepwise selection summary shows which variables were entered into the models as well as the order of entry.

Figure 22: Stepwise Selection Summary

Step	Effect Entered	Effect Removed	Number Effects In	Number Parms In	Model R-Square
			Stepwise Selection Summary		
0	Intercept		1	1	0.0000
1	MomWtGain		2	2	0.0423
2	Mom Smoke		3	3	0.0657
3	Black		4	4	0.0882
4	MomAge		5	5	0.0946

Selection stopped because all effects are in the final model.

All four variables were entered into the model. The last column, labeled Model R-Square, shows the model R-square as each variable is entered into the model.

Important note: The order of entry does not necessarily tell you the relative importance of each variable in predicting the dependent variable. For example, you could have a variable that is highly correlated with the dependent variable but does not enter the model because it was also correlated with other predictor variables that entered first.

One of the default plots shows the value of four different fit methods (Figure 23):

Figure 23: Four Fit Criteria Plots

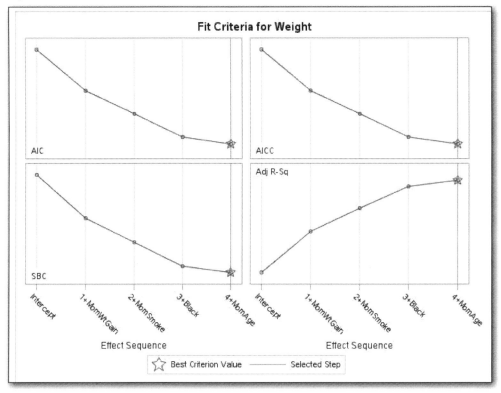

AIC (Akaike's information criteria – yes, I can't pronounce it either!) and a modified version AICC are displayed in the top two graphs. The stars on the plots indicate that the four-variable model is the "best" model as defined by each criterion. The SBC, discussed earlier, is displayed on the bottom left, and the adjusted R-square is displayed on the bottom right. Although all four criteria selected the same model, this is not always the case.

The familiar regression ANOVA table is shown next.

Figure 24: Regression ANOVA Table

Analysis of Variance					
Source	DF	Sum of Squares	Mean Square	F Value	Pr > F
Model	4	373063503	93265876	326.36	<.0001
Error	12495	3570763188	285775		
Corrected Total	12499	3943826691			

The overall *p*-value for this model is quite low. However, remember that there are almost 13,000 observations in the 25% random sample, so even small effects can be significant.

A summary of the fit methods is shown in Figure 25:

Figure 25: R-Square, Adjusted R-Square plus other Measures

Root MSE	534.57962
Dependent Mean	3373.25448
R-Square	0.0946
Adj R-Sq	0.0943
AIC	169544
AICC	169544
SBC	157079

The last portion of the output shows the parameter estimates along with the t and *p*-values. Because there are only two levels of the classification variables, they are easy to interpret. For example, the estimate for Black 0 (non-black) is about 218. This means that after all the other variables are adjusted for; babies of a non-black mother are 218 grams heavier than babies where the mother is black. Because smoking is a risk factor for low birth weight babies, you see that if a mother does not smoke (MomSmoke = 0), the babies are almost 253 grams heavier than if the mother smokes.

Figure 26: Parameter Estimates

		Parameter Estimates			
Parameter	DF	Estimate	Standard Error	t Value	Pr > |t|
Intercept	1	2961.598722	17.629377	167.99	<.0001
MomAge	1	7.963514	0.847390	9.40	<.0001
MomWtGain	1	8.677708	0.374621	23.16	<.0001
Black 0	1	218.282338	13.219116	16.51	<.0001
Black 1	0	0	.	.	.
MomSmoke 0	1	252.807537	14.202584	17.80	<.0001
MomSmoke 1	0	0	.	.	.

Conclusions

As demonstrated in the first multiple regression example, failing to pay attention to the diagnostic information, especially multi-collinearity, can result in models that do not make sense. Besides checking the residuals to see if they are approximately normally distributed and that the variance of the residuals is somewhat homogeneous for different values of your independent variables, there is one additional caution: There is a "rule of thumb" that says you should have approximately 10 times the number of observations as predictor variables in your model. If you have too few observations, you may see very high values of R-square that are simply a mathematical fluke and not actual relationships in your model.

You are probably better off to use a rule of thumb that says something more like: 50 observations plus 10 times the number of independent variables. Also, please keep in mind that having a lot of independent variables makes simple interpretation difficult. Less is truly more in most instances in multiple regression. (Thanks to Jeff Smith for adding this insightful paragraph.)

Problems

11-1: Using the data set SASHELP.Heart, run a simple linear regression with Weight as the dependent variable and Height as the independent or predictor variable. Include a scatter plot of the data. Using the parameter estimates, what is the predicted Weight for a person 65 inches tall?

11-2: Using the data set SASHELP.Heart, run a regression with Weight as the dependent variable and Cholesterol, Systolic, and Sex as predictor variables. Include a panel of diagnostic plots. Because this data set contains over 5,000 observations, be sure to increase the default value of 5,000 for the number of data points to plot. Approximately how much lighter is a female than a male with the same systolic blood pressure and cholesterol?

11-3: Using the data set SASHELP.Heart, run a regression with Weight as the dependent variable and Cholesterol, Systolic, Diastolic, and Sex as predictor variables. Add the option to include the VIR and omit all plots. Rerun this same model using stepwise regression. Accept all the defaults for the decision to add or remove effects. Which of the variables are included in the stepwise model?

11-4: Use the Excel workbook Correlate.xlsx to create a temporary SAS data set called Corr. Run a regression on this data set with z as the dependent variable and x and y as continuous predictor variables. Include the option to print the VIR in the output. Notice the parameter estimates for x and y as well as their *p*-values. It would be instructive to compute a correlation matrix of the three variables x, y, and z using the Correlation analysis task. Return to the regression task and remove y from the model. When you run the model, what can you say about the parameter estimate for x?

Chapter 12: Binary Logistic Regression

Introduction

In the last chapter, you learned how to create multiple regression models. Conceptually, logistic regression has some similarities to multiple regression, although the computational method (maximum likelihood) is quite different (and CPU-intensive). Multiple regression uses a set of predictor variables to predict (and model) a continuous outcome variable. Binary logistic regression uses a set of predictor variables to predict a dichotomous outcome. Theoretically, a multiple regression equation can predict values from negative infinity to positive infinity—binary logistic regression is attempting to compute a probability that an event occurs or does not occur. Because probabilities are bounded between 0 and 1, multiple regression should not be used. Instead, a transformation (called a logit) is performed so that the results of a binary logistic model are bounded by 0 and 1. The transformation, for the mathematically interested reader, is to take the natural log of the odds (the probability that the event occurs divided by the probability that the event does not occur). Luckily, the results of a binary logistic model provide you with odds ratios (OR) for classification variables that have a straightforward interpretation

Preparing the Birth Weight Data Set for Logistic Regression

It is instructive to reanalyze the birth weight data from the last chapter using logistic regression. However, there is one problem: the outcome variable (Weight) in the multiple regression examples was the actual birth weight (in grams). You need to create a dichotomous variable to represent high or low birth weights. (OK, I've just got to tell you this: Speaking of birth weights, our new grandson was born TODAY and he was 7 pounds 13 ounces!)

Instead of using the actual birth weight in grams as the outcome variable, let's create a new variable (call it Wt_Group) that represents weights below and above the median birth weight (3,402 grams). To do this, you need to write a short SAS program. Figure 1 below is such a program. It creates a new, permanent data set called High_Low that contains all the observations from the 25% sample of the SASHELP birth weight data plus the Wt_Group variable.

Figure 1: Program to Create Weight Groups

```
*Program to create a categorical weight variable;
data BOOKDATA.High_Low;
    set Birth_Wt_Sample;
    where Weight is not missing;

    *Wt_Group = 1 is lower weight group
    The median weight is 3402 grams;

    if Weight lt 3402 then Wt_Group = 1;
    else Wt_Group = 0;
run;

title "Listing of First 10 Observations from High_Low";
proc print data=BOOKDATA.High_Low(obs=10);
run;
```

The program starts with a COMMENT statement. COMMENT statements start with an asterisk and end with a semicolon. These statements are ignored when the program executes—they are included to document the program. Next, the DATA statement names the new data set High_Low and uses the libref BOOKDATA to instruct the program to make the data set permanent and place it in the BOOKDATA library.

> When you use a two-level data set name (two names separated by a period), the first part of the name (before the period) is the library name. The second part of the name (after the period) is the data set name.

If you left off the BOOKDATA (and the period), the High_Low data set would be placed in the WORK library. That is fine, except that you would need to re-create it every time you opened a new Studio session.

SAS uses a SET statement to read observations from another SAS data set. This SET statement says to read observations from the Birth_Wt_Sample data set, the same data set that was created with the Random selection task in Chapter 9.

Because you want to eliminate any observation in the input data set (Birth_Wt_Sample), where the variable Weight is a missing value, you add a WHERE statement to delete such observations. (Note: There are no observations with missing birth weights in the SASHELP data set, but it is always a good idea to test for missing values in a SAS program.) The WHERE statement in this program uses the keywords IS NOT MISSING to test for missing values of Weight. If Weight is not missing, the program continues—if Weight is missing, the statement is not true and the program returns to the top of the DATA step to read the next observation.

There is another COMMENT statement telling anyone reading this program that Wt_Group = 1 includes the low birth weight babies (a possible risk factor). The IF statement tests if the variable Weight is less than (abbreviated LT) 3,402. If the logical expression in the IF statement is true, the expression following the logical comparison is executed. So, in this case, if Weight is less than 3,402, Wt_Group is set to 1; otherwise, it is set to 0.

> The reason that the program did not include observations where the variable Weight was a missing value is that missing values in SAS are logically lower than any real value. If you had missing values and did not eliminate or test for them, the expression `if Weight LT 3402` would be true for missing values. That is, missing values are less than any real value.

The DATA step ends with a RUN statement. You are actually done now, but it is always a good idea to take a look at the first few observations in a data set to be sure the program runs as you expected. You could have used the List data task in SAS Studio, but it was just as easy to include a procedure to print the first few observations in the new data set. You use a DATA= data set option to tell PROC PRINT that you want to print observations from the BOOKDATA.High_Low data set. The OBS=10 in parentheses following the data set name is a data set option, and it says to stop printing when you reach observation 10.

This program was run and the output is shown in Figure 2:

Figure 2: Listing of the First 10 Observations in Data Set High_Low

Listing of First 10 Observations from High_Low

Obs	Weight	Black	Married	Boy	MomAge	MomSmoke	CigsPerDay	MomWtGain	Visit	MomEdLevel	Wt_Group
1	3430	1	1	1	-4	0	0	-6	3	0	0
2	3657	0	1	0	6	0	0	15	3	0	0
3	4054	0	1	1	-5	0	0	21	3	2	0
4	4536	1	0	1	3	0	0	-1	3	3	0
5	3295	0	1	1	6	0	0	-29	3	2	1
6	3458	0	1	1	8	0	0	-18	3	1	0
7	3714	0	0	1	2	0	0	25	1	1	0
8	2807	0	1	0	-5	1	1	13	3	0	1
9	3625	0	1	0	2	0	0	0	3	0	0
10	3884	0	1	1	-2	0	0	-10	3	0	0

Notice the last column of this listing. This column contains the new Wt_Group variable. You are now ready to run a binary logistic regression model. Start by selecting Binary logistic regression from the task list. Select the BOOKDATA.High_Low data set, and select Wt_Group as your response variable. In addition, you can select which event (in this case, 0 – above the median or 1 – below the median) you want to predict. Although most of the birth weights in this data set are not extremely low, choosing event = 1 (low birth weight) seems to make the most sense (see Figure 3 below):

Figure 3: Selecting a Response Variable and Event of Interest

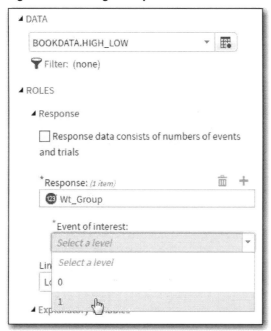

The next step is to select classification (categorical) variables and choose a Coding method. For all the examples in this book, Reference coding is used. Reference coding, the most popular coding method, at least in the health sciences, computes statistics such as odds ratios, based on a reference level. For this first demonstration of binary logistic regression, you are going to allow the procedure to select a reference level. In a later section, you will see how to choose the reference level yourself.

The two variables, Black (1=black, 0=non-black) and MomSmoke (1=yes, 0=no), are good candidates for classification variables (Figure 4):

Figure 4: Selecting Classification Variables and Reference Coding

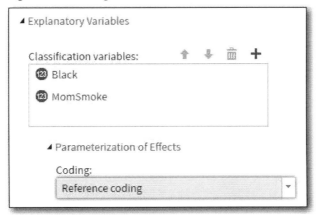

Next, add MomWtGain and MomAge as continuous variables (not shown).

Click the Model tab to specify your model. This process is similar to the way you specified a model for multiple regression. First, click Edit. Next, highlight the four variables on the top left-side of the screen. Finally, click Add and then OK (Figure 5):

Figure 5: Specifying your Model

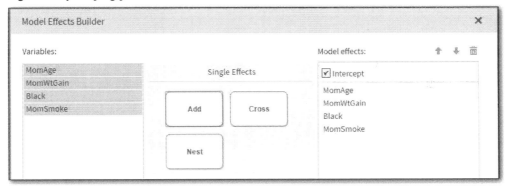

At this point, use the default values for the remaining options and selection criteria, and run the task. There is a lot of output, so we'll discuss it piece by piece.

To start, you will see model information; numbers of observations read and used (pay careful attention to these, especially if there are a lot fewer observations used than read); a table showing values of your response variable (Wt_Group); and the fact that you are modeling Wt_Group = 1 (low birth weight).

Figure 6: Model Information and Response Profile

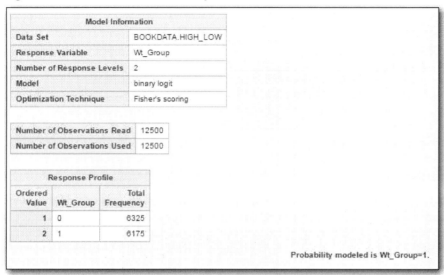

Next, there is a table showing your classification variables and their values. Make sure that these values are what you expect. A single data error can result in extra levels of these variables and invalidate the entire process.

Figure 7: Class Level Information

Class Level Information		
Class	Value	Design Variables
Black	0	1
	1	0
Mom Smoke	0	1
	1	0

Everything is as you expected, with values of 0 and 1 for both variables.

The next section of output shows model fit statistics. These are a bit complicated and are more useful when comparing models. Smaller values of AIC (Akaike's information criteria) indicate better models. The criterion labeled SC (Schwarz Criterion) is based on the value of AIC but adjusts for the number of variables entered into the model. As with AIC, smaller values of SC indicate better models. The Schwarz Criterion is probably better to use than the AIC if you want a parsimonious model (fewer predictor variables).

Figure 8: Fit Statistics

Model Fit Statistics		
Criterion	Intercept Only	Intercept and Covariates
AIC	17328.879	16490.398
SC	17336.313	16527.565
-2 Log L	17326.879	16480.398

Next comes the global test of the null hypothesis. If this is not significant, it may be back to the drawing board. Here, three tests of the null hypothesis all reject it with very low *p*-values.

Figure 9: Test of Global Null Hypothesis

Testing Global Null Hypothesis: BETA=0			
Test	Chi-Square	DF	Pr > ChiSq
Likelihood Ratio	846.4819	4	<.0001
Score	816.2735	4	<.0001
Wald	761.0124	4	<.0001

The *p*-values for each of the predictor variables (both classification variables and continuous variables) are presented (Figure 10):

Figure 10: p-Values for Effects

Type 3 Analysis of Effects			
Effect	DF	Wald Chi-Square	Pr > ChiSq
MomAge	1	83.0882	<.0001
MomWtGain	1	291.4380	<.0001
Black	1	183.9687	<.0001
MomSmoke	1	210.9599	<.0001

All variables are significant. Now comes the important information on the predictor variables: the odds ratios. The odds ratios for the two classification variables are easier to understand, and we will look at them first. For Black (0 versus 1), you see a point estimate of .491. Because you didn't select a reference level for the two classification variables, the task selected the higher value (1) as the reference level (Figure 11):

Figure 11: Odds Ratios

		95% Wald	
Effect	Point Estimate	Confidence Limits	
MomAge	0.970	0.964	0.977
MomWtGain	0.975	0.972	0.978
Black 0 vs 1	0.491	0.443	0.544
MomSmoke 0 vs 1	0.436	0.389	0.487

Because the odds ratio for Black is .491, you conclude that a person who is non-black (0) is less likely to have a baby whose weight is below the median value. If you take the reciprocal of this value (about 2.037), it is easier to interpret. You could say, based on this model, that the odds of a black mother having a baby whose weight is below the median is 2.038 times higher than for a non-black mother. The 95% confidence limits indicate that you are 95% confident that your estimate of the odds ratio is between those two limits. Because both classification variables were significant, these limits do not include 1 (meaning that the odds are equal for each outcome). The same interpretation holds for the mother smoking or not. The value .436 means that non-smoking moms are less likely to have babies with birth weights below the median.

The odds ratios for the continuous variables show the odds for each year (for MomAge) or each pound (for MomWtGain). There are options in PROC LOGISTIC for changing these odds ratios so that they represent the odds ratios for multiples of each continuous variable. (See Cody 2011 for more details.) For example, you might want to know the odds ratio that corresonds to 10-pound changes instead of 1-pound changes.

Selecting Reference Levels for Your Model

It is quite easy to modify the program produced by the Binary logistic task to specify reference levels for your classification variables. First, click the Edit icon in the Code window. All you need to do is add a reference level for each variable listed in the CLASS statement. In the program shown in Figure 12, a reference level of 0 was selected for the two variables Black and MomSmoke. Notice that this level is placed in quotations marks. The reason for the quotation marks is a bit complicated. (See Cody 2011, *SAS Statistics by Example* for a complete explanation or just use the quotation marks.)

Figure 12: Editing the Program to Specify Reference Levels

```
proc logistic data=BOOKDATA.HIGH_LOW plots
    (maxpoints=none)=(oddsratio(cldisplay=serifarrow) roc);
  class Black(ref='0') MomSmoke(ref='0') / param=ref;
  model Wt_Group(event='1')=MomAge MomWtGain Black MomSmoke/
      link=logit
      technique=fisher;
run;
```

Running the program again with the reference levels specified, results in the odds ratios showing the risk for a black mother or a mother who smokes compared to a non-black mother or a non-smoking mother. Notice that the new odds ratios are the reciprocals of the odds ratios where the reference level was 1 instead of 0. See Figure 13 below:

Figure 13: New Odds Ratios

Odds Ratio Estimates			
Effect	Point Estimate	95% Wald Confidence Limits	
MomAge	0.970	0.964	0.977
MomWtGain	0.975	0.972	0.978
Black 1 vs 0	2.038	1.839	2.259
MomSmoke 1 vs 0	2.295	2.052	2.567

Conclusions

Programming a logistic regression model by writing the actual SAS code is a bit daunting. However, by using the Binary logistic regression task, it is quite easy to do. This is one instance where even a veteran programmer may decide that a point-and-click approach to running this task is a good choice.

Problems

12-1: Starting with the SASHELP data set Heart, run a binary logistic regression with Status as the Response variable and Dead as the event of interest. Select the two variables Chol_Status (cholesterol status) and BP_Status (blood pressure status) as classification variables. Create a filter using the expression:

```
BP_Status ne 'Optimal'
```

Set parameterization of effects to Reference.

12-2: Run problem 12-1 again except edit the code so that the reference level for Chol_Status is 'Desirable' and the reference level for BP_Status is 'Normal'. Compare the odds ratio to the previous result.

12-3: Starting with the CSV file Risk.csv, create a temporary SAS data set (call it Risk). Use the binary logistic regression task to predict a heart attack (variable Heart_Attack, 1=yes, 0=no) with the two risk factors Age_Group (Less than 60, 61 to 70, and 71 and older) and Chol_High (1=yes, 0=no). Use reference coding.

12-4: Repeat problem 12-3, but set the reference level for Age_Group = '1:Less 60' and for Chol_High = '0'.

Chapter 13: Analyzing Categorical Data

Introduction

Quite a bit of data used in the health sciences deals with frequency counts and proportions. For example, you may have data from a cohort study where one group of subjects has high cholesterol and another group has low or normal levels of cholesterol. You then follow these groups and count number of heart attacks that occur in each group after a predetermined period of time. One of your goals would be to determine if the proportion of subjects who had heart attacks (myocardial infarctions, in doctor-speak) was higher in the high-cholesterol group. Remember, that even if there were no relationship between cholesterol level and heart attack (a good choice of a null hypothesis for this study), there could still be differences in the incidence of heart attacks in the two groups that make up your sample data. You need to determine if the difference that you observe has a low probability of occurring if the null hypothesis is true.

This chapter covers tests to compare proportions, as in the hypothetical example stated here, and other tests of association.

Describing the Heart_Attack Data Set

Many of the examples in this chapter use a data set called Heart_Attack. A screen shot of the worksheet containing the data is shown in Figure 1. (Note: This data set was generated for instructional purposes and is not actual data.)

Figure 1: First Few Rows in the Heart_Attack Worksheet

	A	B	C	D	E	F
1	Gender	Age	Age_Group	Chol	High_Chol	Heart_Attack
2	F	63	2	211	1	0
3	M	69	2	249	1	0
4	F	69	2	139	0	0
5	M	59	1	239	1	0
6	F	71	3	195	0	0
7	M	50	1	193	0	0
8	F	57	1	179	0	0
9	M	75	3	186	0	1
10	F	60	2	164	0	0
		52		237		

The information in this file is coded as follows:

Variable Name	Description	Values
Gender	Gender of Subject	F=Female, M=Male
Age	Age in years	
Age_Group	Age Group	1=<60, 2=60-70, 3=71 and older
Chol	Total Cholesterol	
High_Chol	Is Cholesterol level high?	1=Yes, 0=No
Heart_Attack	Did subject have a heart attack?	1=Yes, 0=No

Besides looking at simple frequencies for variables such as Gender, Age_Group, High_Chol, and Heart_Attack, you will also want to examine risk factors for heart attacks by generating two-way tables. Because the variable Heart_Attack has only two values, you could also use binary logistic regression (described in the previous chapter) to explore the relationship between risk factors and heart attacks.

Computing One-Way Frequencies

Before you can use SAS Studio to analyze this data set, you need to use the Import Utility to convert the workbook into a SAS data set. As a reminder:

Tasks and Utilities ▶ Utilities ▶ Import Data

This process was used to create a SAS data set called Heart_Attack that was stored in the BOOKDATA library. The listing in Figure 2 was created by using the List Data task (with the option to list the first 10 observations):

Figure 2: First 10 Observations in the SAS Data Set Heart_Attack

Obs	Gender	Age	Age_Group	Chol	High_Chol	Heart_Attack
1	F	63	2	211	1	0
2	M	69	2	249	1	0
3	F	69	2	139	0	0
4	M	59	1	239	1	0
5	F	71	3	195	0	0
6	M	50	1	193	0	0
7	F	57	1	179	0	0
8	M	75	3	186	0	1
9	F	60	2	164	0	0
10	M	52	1	237	1	1

To compute one-way frequencies, double-click One-Way Frequencies in the statistics task list, to bring up the following screen (Figure 3):

Figure 3: Demonstrating the One-Way Frequency Task

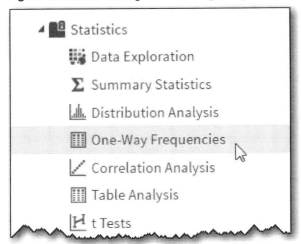

Next, enter information on the Data tab (Figure 4):

Figure 4: Data Tab Selections

Choose the Heart_Attack data set stored in the permanent BOOKDATA library on the Data tab. Next, select the variables Gender, Age_Group, High_Chol, and Heart_Attack in the Analysis variables box.

Before you run the procedure, click the Options tab to select additional options (Figure 5):

Figure 5: One-Way Frequencies Options

In this example, you have chosen to suppress plots and to deselect the default option to include cumulative frequencies and percentages. You are now ready to run the procedure. The output is shown in Figure 6:

Figure 6: Frequency Tables

The FREQ Procedure

Gender		
Gender	Frequency	Percent
F	250	50.00
M	250	50.00

Age_Group		
Age_Group	Frequency	Percent
1	146	29.20
2	180	36.00
3	174	34.80

High_Chol		
High_Chol	Frequency	Percent
0	245	49.00
1	255	51.00

Heart_Attack		
Heart_Attack	Frequency	Percent
0	442	88.40
1	58	11.60

You see the frequency and percent for each unique value of these variables. Although this is useful information, it could be improved by replacing the values of Age_Group (1,2,3), Gender (F,M), and the two variables High_Chol and Heart_Attack (0,1) with labels. You can define formats to associate each of these unique values with labels. That is the topic of the next section.

Creating Formats

You will need to write a few lines of SAS code to create the formats that you will use to label the values in these tables. You create formats with a SAS procedure called PROC FORMAT. Figure 7 is a program that creates three formats and then creates a copy of the Heart_Attack data set where these formats are associated with the appropriate variables.

Figure 7: Adding Formats to the Data Set

```
*Adding formats to the Heart_Attack Dataset;

proc format;  ①
   value $gender 'F' = 'Female'  ②
                 'M' = 'Male';
   value Yesno 0 = 'No'  ③
               1 = 'Yes';
   value Age_Group 1 = '< 60'  ④
                   2 = '60-70'
                   3 = '71+';
run;

data Heart_Attack;  ⑤
   set bookdata.Heart_Attack;  ⑥
   format Gender $Gender.  ⑦
          Heart_Attack High_Chol Yesno.
          Age_Group Age_Group.;
run;

title "Listing the First 10 Observations from Heart_Attack";
proc print data=Heart_Attack(obs=10);  ⑧
run;
```

The first line of the program is a comment statement stating the purpose of the program. Remember that comment statements start with an asterisk and end with a semicolon.

① PROC FORMAT is used to create SAS formats.

② Use a VALUE statement to define each format that you want to create. Follow the keyword VALUE with a format name. Format names are a maximum of 32 characters and must contain only letters, digits, and the underscore character. One additional rule is that format names cannot end in a digit. Finally, if the format is to be used with character data (such as Gender), you use a dollar sign as the first character in the format name. (Note: the $ character counts as one of the 32 characters in the format name.) Although the format $Gender is going to be used with the variable called Gender, the format name can be anything you want. It could have been named $Oscar.

Following the format name, you define labels for each value that you wish to label. Because Gender is a character variable, the values 'M' and 'F' must be in single or double quotation marks. Following each value (or a list of values separated by commas), you type an equal sign and the format label. This label also belongs in single or double quotation marks.

You can read more about how to create formats in several of the SAS Press books including *Learning SAS by Example* (Cody, 2007) or An *Introduction to SAS University Edition* (Cody, 2015).

③ The Yesno format will be used for the two variables High_Chol and Heart_Attack. Because these variables are numeric, the format name does not start with a $.

④ The last format will be used to label the three Age_Group values.

⑤ The DATA statement is creating a new data set called Heart_Attack. Because this data set name does not contain a period, this data set is a temporary data set and will be stored in the WORK library. You could have also used WORK.Heart_Attack for the data set name.

⑥ The SET statement reads observations from an existing SAS data set. Essentially, this makes a copy of the permanent data set BOOKDATA.Heart_Attack and creates a temporary SAS data set with the same name. The only difference is that the new temporary data set will include the associations between certain variables and formats because of the FORMAT statement in the next line.

⑦ The FORMAT statement associates variable names and formats. In this format statement, the format $Gender will be used to format the variable Gender. Notice the period following the format name. This tells the DATA step that $Gender is a format and not a variable name. Because the format Yesno is going to be used with the two variables, Heart_Attack and High_Chol, you list both of these variables and follow them with the format name Yesno. Again, notice that there is a period after the format name. Finally, the format Age_Group is associated with the variable Age_Group. You end the DATA step with a RUN statement.

⑧ PROC PRINT is used to list the first 10 observations in the new data set Heart_Attack. As an alternative, you could use the List Data task to list these observations. The listing is displayed in Figure 8:

Figure 8: First 10 Observations from Data Set Heart_Attack (with formats)

Listing the First 10 Observations from Heart_Attack

Obs	Gender	Age	Age_Group	Chol	High_Chol	Heart_Attack
1	Female	63	60-70	211	Yes	No
2	Male	69	60-70	249	Yes	No
3	Female	69	60-70	139	No	No
4	Male	59	< 60	239	Yes	No
5	Female	71	71+	195	No	No
6	Male	50	< 60	193	No	No
7	Female	57	< 60	179	No	No
8	Male	75	71+	186	No	Yes
9	Female	60	60-70	164	No	No
10	Male	52	< 60	237	Yes	Yes

Notice that the formats that you created are displayed in this listing. Because the association between the variables and formats was executed in a DATA step, this association will be maintained in other SAS procedures such as the one-way or two-way tables.

It is important to remember that the actual values for the formatted variables still exist in the SAS data set. The formats labels only appear when you use certain procedures that present data, such as the listing above or the tables that you will be producing in this chapter.

Producing One-Way Tables with Formats

If you rerun one-way frequencies (see Figure 6) with the WORK data set Heart_Attack (the one with associated formats), the one-way frequency tables will now display formatted values. Only two tables (for the variables Age_Group and Heart_Attack) are shown here in Figure 9:

Figure 9: One-Way Frequencies with Formatted Values

The FREQ Procedure

Age_Group	Frequency	Percent
< 60	146	29.20
60-70	180	36.00
71+	174	34.80

Heart_Attack	Frequency	Percent
No	442	88.40
Yes	58	11.60

These tables have a clear advantage over the unformatted tables produced earlier. For example, it saves you the trouble of going back to your coding scheme to see what age groups 1, 2, and 3 represent. Take a moment to look at the table showing frequencies for heart attacks. Notice that the values (No followed by Yes) are in the same order as in the original unformatted table. The reason for this is that the One_Way task orders values in a frequency table by the internal values of the variables. Because the original values were 0 (No) and 1 (Yes), the table is displayed with 'No' as the first category listed, followed by 'Yes'. You will see how to change the order of values in one-way frequencies tables or in 2-by-2 tables later in this chapter. (I know you excited about this, but just hold on a minute.)

Creating Two-Way Tables

To see relationships between variables, such as if high levels of cholesterol increase the incidence of heart attacks, you will want to produce two-way tables. The first step is to double-click Table Analysis in the statistics task menu (Figure 10):

Figure 10: Creating a Two-Way Table

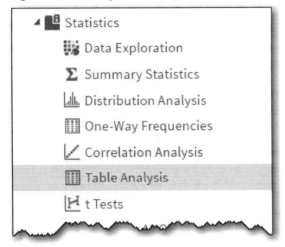

Next fill in the Data tab.

Figure 11: Completing the Data Tab for Two-Way Table

Notice that the Heart_Attack data set in the WORK library (the one with formats) is selected as the data source. Next, you get to choose which variables form the rows of the table and which variables form the columns. Every variable selected in the Row variables box will be paired with every variable in the Column variables box. It is typical to choose the outcome variable (in this case, having a heart attack or not) as a column variable and the other variables such as High_Chol as row variables.

There are many more options to choose from in the Table task compared to the One-Way task. Click the Options tab to get started (see Figure 12):

Figure 12: Options for the Two-Way Table

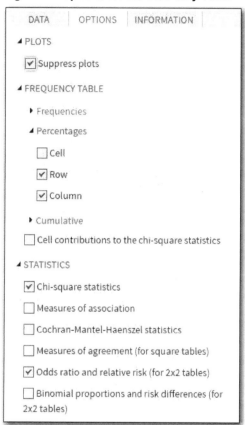

Check Suppress plots if you do not want plots. Next, you have a choice of what percentages you would like to display. Here, you have chosen to see row and column percentages. Because you don't want to see cumulative frequencies (not usually useful), make sure that this box is unchecked.

As you can see, there are many options in the statistics menu. Two of the more common options, Chi-square and Odds ratios and relative risks (also known as risk ratios), were chosen for this example. It's time to run the task. Here are the results. (Note: to save space, only one table was included here. You can see a display that includes odds ratios and relative risks later in Figure 19 in this chapter.)

Figure 13: Table of Cholesterol Level versus Heart Attack

Frequency Row Pct Col Pct	Table of High_Chol by Heart_Attack		
		Heart_Attack(Heart_Attack)	
High_Chol(High_Chol)	No	Yes	Total
No	231 94.29 52.26	14 5.71 24.14	245
Yes	211 82.75 47.74	44 17.25 75.86	255
Total	442	58	500

The box in the upper-left corner of the output is the key to the three numbers in each box. The top number is a frequency count. For example, there were 231 subjects who did not have high cholesterol and who did not have a heart attack. The second number in each cell is a row percentage. In this example, 94.29% of the subjects who did not have high cholesterol did not have a heart attack. Finally, the third number in each cell is a column percentage: 52.26% of the subjects who did not have a heart attack also did not have high cholesterol.

Although all the information you need is included in this table, it is preferable to rearrange the order of values in the rows and columns so that the first column is Yes (had a heart attack) and the top row is Yes (had high cholesterol). You can use formats (plus an added option of PROC FREQ, the procedure that produces these tables) to reorder the rows and columns.

Using Formats to Reorder the Rows and Columns of a Table

There is an option in PROC FREQ called ORDER= that allows you to select several ways to order values in a table. The default order is by internal value. That is why the tables printed so far placed 'No' before 'Yes', 0 before 1, and the age groups in order from 1 to 3. You can set ORDER=Formatted to request that the values in a table are ordered by the formatted values rather than the non-formatted (internal) values.

The program shown in Figure 14 uses a trick that is popular with SAS programmers: The formats are written to force the values for 'Yes' to come before the values for 'No' and for "Male" to come before 'Female'. Here is the program:

Figure 14: Rewriting the Formats

```
*Adding formats to the Heart_Attack Dataset;

proc format;
   value $gender 'F' = '2:Female'
                 'M' = '1:Male';
   value Yesno 0 = '2:No'
               1 = '1:Yes';
   value Age_Group 1 = '< 60'
                   2 = '60-70'
```

```
                        3 = '71+';
   run;

   data Heart_Attack;
      set bookdata.Heart_Attack;
      format Gender $Gender.
             Heart_Attack High_Chol Yesno.
             Age_Group Age_Group.;
   run;
```

The numbers (1 and 2) as part of the format labels for the two formats $Gender and Yesno, force
the tables to be ordered the way you prefer. (Even though '1' and '2' are digits, '1' comes before '2'
alphabetically.) By the way, the three labels for the Age_Group format are already in alphabetical
order, so there is no need to add digits to these format labels. There is one more thing to do
before you create the tables. You need to edit the SAS code produced by the Tables task to add
the option ORDER=Formatted. Once you have filled out the Data and Options tables with your
preferences, click the Edit icon in the code window (Figure 15):

Figure 15: Editing the Code Generated by the Tables Task

Now you can add the ORDER=Formatted option like this:

Figure 16: Adding the ORDER= Option to PROC FREQ

```
proc freq data=WORK.Heart_ATTACK order=formatted;
   tables (High_Chol) * (Heart_Attack) / chisq relrisk nopercent
      nocum plots=none;
run;
```

Now, click the Run icon. The table is now in the preferred order (see Figure 17):

Figure 17: New Two-Way Table with Order Changed

Frequency Row Pct Col Pct	Table of High_Chol by Heart_Attack			
		Heart_Attack(Heart_Attack)		
High_Chol(High_Chol)		1:Yes	2:No	Total
1:Yes		44 17.25 75.86	211 82.75 47.74	255
2:No		14 5.71 24.14	231 94.29 52.26	245
Total		58	442	500

The top left cell represents subjects who have high cholesterol and who also had a heart attack.

The table statistics are displayed in Figure 18:

Figure 18: Table Statistics

Statistics for Table of High_Chol by Heart_Attack

Statistic	DF	Value	Prob
Chi-Square	1	16.2287	<.0001
Likelihood Ratio Chi-Square	1	17.0012	<.0001
Continuity Adj. Chi-Square	1	15.1228	0.0001
Mantel-Haenszel Chi-Square	1	16.1963	<.0001
Phi Coefficient		0.1802	
Contingency Coefficient		0.1773	
Cramer's V		0.1802	

The value of Chi-square and the *p*-values are the same as before. So, why was it so important to change the order of the rows and columns in the table? The answer is that the odds ratios and relative risks for the relationship between cholesterol and heart attack now show the risk of having a heart attack if you have high cholesterol (Figure 19):

Figure 19: Odds Ratio and Relative Risk

Odds Ratio and Relative Risks			
Statistic	Value	95% Confidence Limits	
Odds Ratio	3.4408	1.8331	6.4580
Relative Risk (Column 1)	3.0196	1.6987	5.3678
Relative Risk (Column 2)	0.8776	0.8232	0.9356

Remember that the program doesn't know if you conducted a case-control study (where you use the Odds Ratio) or a cohort study (where you will use the Relative risk). Because this was a cohort study, you can report that a person is 3.0196 times more likely to suffer a heart attack if he or she has high cholesterol. The table also shows the confidence limits for the odds ratio and relative risks. Notice that these intervals do not include 1. An odds ratio or relative risk of 1 would mean that a person with high cholesterol was not at a higher or lower risk of having a heart attack. You expect this because of the significant chi-square value.

Although it is not shown here, running the Tables task with the new formats places 'Male' before 'Female' for the columns and 'Yes' before 'No' on the rows. The resulting relative risk (about 1.5) is the increased risk for a heart attack for males compared to females.

Computing Chi-Square from Frequency Data

When you already have a 2-by-2 table with frequency counts, you can still use the Table analysis task to compute chi-square and related statistics. Suppose you already have a table with the data from Figure 13. You can put the data from this table in an Excel worksheet as follows:

Figure 20: Worksheet Containing Counts

	A	B	C
1	Row	Col	Count
2	1	1	44
3	1	2	211
4	2	1	14
5	2	2	231

The next step is to convert this data into a SAS data set using the Import utility. Figure 22 (below) is a listing of the SAS data set created from the frequency data. The WORK data set was called Counts.

Figure 21: Data Imported into a SAS Data Set

List Data for WORK.COUNTS

Obs	Row	Col	Count
1	1	1	44
2	1	2	211
3	2	1	14
4	2	2	231

Start the Table analysis task and use the Data tab to identify the variable Row as the row variable and the variable Col as the column variable.

Figure 22: Table Analysis Data Tab

In order to tell the task that you already have frequency data, click Additional Roles at the bottom of the Data screen (Figure 23.

Figure 23: Identifying the Variable Representing Frequencies

Click the plus sign and select the variable Count as the variable that represents the frequency data. Finally, select the Options tab and select the statistics that you want. Because this data is the same as presented in this chapter, only the 2-by-2 table is shown (below), so you can see that starting from frequency data results in the same table when you had raw data.

Figure 24: Resulting Table

Frequency Row Pct Col Pct	Table of Row by Col		
		Col(Col)	
Row(Row)	1	2	Total
1	44 17.25 75.86	211 82.75 47.74	255
2	14 5.71 24.14	231 94.29 52.26	245
Total	58	442	500

Analyzing Tables with Low Expected Values

The final topic in this chapter deals with 2-by-2 tables with expected values less than 5. You may recall that one of the assumptions for computing chi-square in a 2-by-2 table is that all of the expected values are 5 or more. When this is not the case, a popular alternative to chi-square is Fisher's Exact test.

There are statisticians who prefer chi-square with a correction for continuity instead of Fisher's Exact test. SAS produces both statistics, so you can take your pick.

Let's use the table displayed in Figure 25 to demonstrate how to analyze tables with small expected values.

Figure 25: Table with Expected Values Less than 5

Table of Row by Column			
	Column		
Row	1	2	Total
1	2	10	12
2	7	4	11
Total	9	14	23

Remember that the 2-by-2 frequency table displayed in Figure 25 contains actual counts, not expected values. You can easily compute the expected value for each cell or let SAS do it. Let's do the latter. You can click the Data tab and check the box to display expected values. This adds expected values to each cell. It looks like this:

Figure 26: Displaying Expected Values for Each Cell

Frequency Expected	Table of Row by Column		
		Column	
	Row	1	2	Total
	1	2	10	12
		4.6957	7.3043	
	2	7	4	11
		4.3043	6.6957	
	Total	9	14	23

The bottom number in each cell is the expected value for that cell. Notice that two cells have expected values less than 5. To perform Fisher's Exact test, click Exact Test on the Options tab and check the box for Fisher's Exact test (Figure 27):

Figure 27: Selecting Fisher's Exact Test

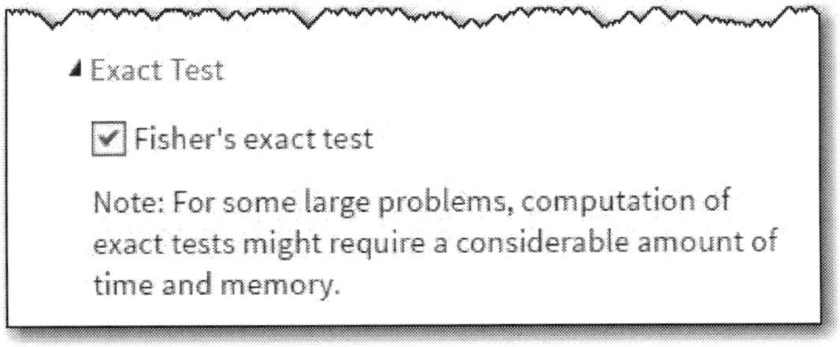

◢ Exact Test

☑ Fisher's exact test

Note: For some large problems, computation of exact tests might require a considerable amount of time and memory.

It's time to run the task. Figure 28 and Figure 29 show values for the continuity adjusted chi-square (3.5267, p = .0604) and Fisher's Exact test (two-sided value p = .0361):

Figure 28: Chi=Square and Adjusted Chi-Square

Statistics for Table of Row by Column			
Statistic	DF	Value	Prob
Chi-Square	1	5.3158	0.0211
Likelihood Ratio Chi-Square	1	5.5550	0.0184
Continuity Adj. Chi-Square	1	3.5267	0.0604
Mantel-Haenszel Chi-Square	1	5.0847	0.0241
Phi Coefficient		-0.4808	
Contingency Coefficient		0.4333	
Cramer's V		-0.4808	
WARNING: 50% of the cells have expected counts less than 5. Chi-Square may not be a valid test.			

Figure 29: Fisher's Exact Test

Fisher's Exact Test	
Cell (1,1) Frequency (F)	2
Left-sided Pr <= F	0.0291
Right-sided Pr >= F	0.9975
Table Probability (P)	0.0267
Two-sided Pr <= P	0.0361

Conclusions

Analysis of frequency data is one of the major tools in analyzing health outcomes where the recorded values are dichotomous or ordinal in nature. The two tasks, One-Way Frequencies and Table Analysis, provide you with all the tools you need. In addition, this chapter showed you how to create formats and to use formats to control the order of values in one-way or two-way tables

Problems

13-1: Starting with the file Risk.csv, use the import utility to create a temporary SAS data set called Risk. Use the One-way Frequencies task to create one-way frequencies for the variables Age_Group, Chol_High, Gender, and Heart_Attack. Use the appropriate options to omit plots and to omit cumulative frequencies and percentages.

13-2: Using the SAS data set Risk from problem 13-1, construct a 2 x 2 table with the variable Chol_High on the row dimension and Heart_Attack on the column dimension. Include a calculation of chi-square, odds ratio, and relative risk. Omit all plots.

13-3: Repeat problem 13-2 except add the necessary statements (and edit the task) so that column 1 is Heart_attack = 1 and row 1 is Chol_High = 1.

13-4: Given the table below, create a SAS data set and compute chi-square for the table. What is the odds ratio for the risk factor = Yes?

Table of Risk_Factor by Outcome

Risk_Factor   Outcome

Frequency	Bad	Good	Total
1-Yes	50	15	65
2-No	25	40	65
Total	75	55	130

13-5: Given the table below, compute Fisher's exact test and the continuity-corrected chi-square:

Table of Risk_Factor by Outcome

Risk_Factor   Outcome

Frequency	Bad	Good	Total
1-Yes	5	3	8
2-No	2	15	17
Total	7	18	25

Chapter 14: Computing Power and Sample Size

Introduction

In my 26 years as a biostatistician at the Rutgers Robert Wood Johnson Medical School in New Jersey, the most frequent question I was asked was "I'm doing an experiment, how many subjects do I need?" Just about any study, especially one for which you are asking for funding or applying for a grant, will require detailed power and sample size calculations.

For those readers a bit rusty on this subject, the power of a study is the probability that the study will result in a statistically significant finding if the drug or treatment that you are studying is different (hopefully better) than either a placebo or an alternate drug or treatment. For many studies conducted at research labs or universities, powers of 80% or 90% are typical. Very large-scale studies may strive for a power of 95%. Small exploratory studies may be satisfied with powers closer to 70%. The bottom line is that it is unethical and wasteful to begin a study with low power. You will have a low probability of demonstrating the superiority of your drug or intervention, and this negative result may dissuade others from investigating the same drug or intervention when it may actually be beneficial.

Depending on the type of study (comparing means or comparing proportions, for example), there is a set of questions that need to be answered before you can determine the number of subjects you will need for a particular study. SAS Studio includes a Power and Sample Size task that performs this analysis for many of the popular study designs.

Computing Sample Size for a t Test

Let's start with a simple study to compare blood pressure in a group of borderline hypertensive subjects. You want to see if a low dose of a beta blocker will reduce blood pressure. Because these subjects are borderline hypertensive and the trial will be relatively short, you decide that it is ethical to use a placebo as your control.

What information do you need to decide how many subjects you need to recruit in order to have a power of 80%? Let's open up the Power and Sample Size tab. It looks like this:

Figure 1: Power and Sample Size Menu

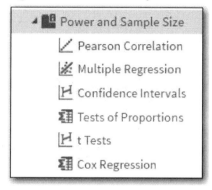

Use the t Tests selection to begin the sample size calculation for comparing two means. Double-clicking t Tests brings up the following:

Figure 2: Select Type of Test and Sample Size or Power

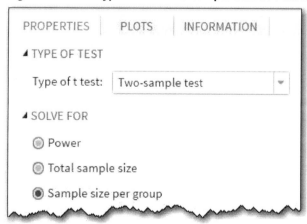

The pull-down list under Type of *t* test allows you to select from a one-sample test or a two-sample test (either paired or unpaired). Because your study design called for two unpaired groups, select the two-sample option. Next, you can choose to compute power (for a given sample size) or sample size (for a given power). In addition, you can request the total sample size or the sample size per group. It is the latter choice that is shown in Figure 2.

The next section of the Properties tab asks you to decide if the test is one or two-sided. Most studies of this type are two-sided. You can also decide if you want to assume equal variances in the two groups. Figure 3 shows selections for a two-sided test with equal (pooled) variances.

Figure 3: Select Distribution, 1- or 2-Tailed, and Variance Assumption

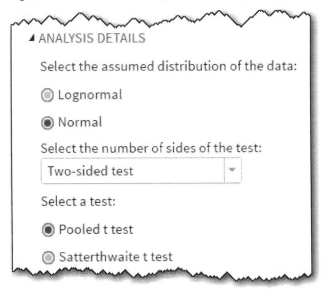

The calculation for power requires you to either estimate the means of the two groups or the difference between the two means. The screen shot in Figure 4 shows the different ways that you can enter this information.

Figure 4: Select Ways to Specify Means or Differences

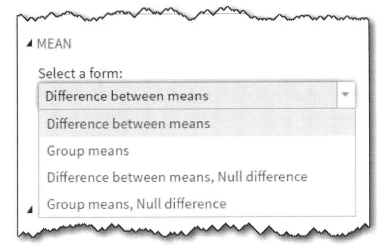

For this example, you are choosing to enter the group means you expect. With this selection, the menu system opens boxes for you to enter the expected mean for each group (Figure 5):

Figure 5: Entering Means for Each Group

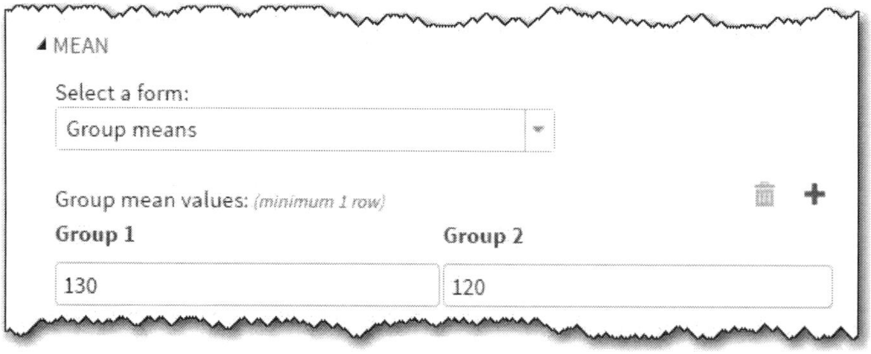

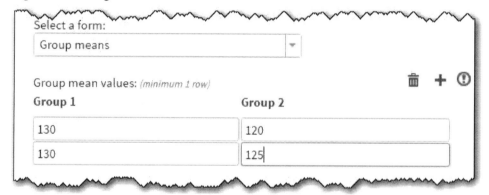

By clicking the plus sign above the location where you enter your choices for means, you can calculate sample size for different choices of sample means. Figure 6 shows that you want to compute sample sizes for means of 130 versus 120 (a 10-point difference) and 130 versus 125 (a 5-point difference).

Figure 6: Entering Another Pair of Means

Your final two decisions are to estimate the standard deviation and the desired power. As with other choices in this task, you can enter several selections for each. In Figure 7, you see an estimate of 10 for the standard deviation and two powers: .8 and .9. Note that powers are entered as probabilities (values between 0 and 1) and not as percentages.

Figure 7: Enter the Desired Power

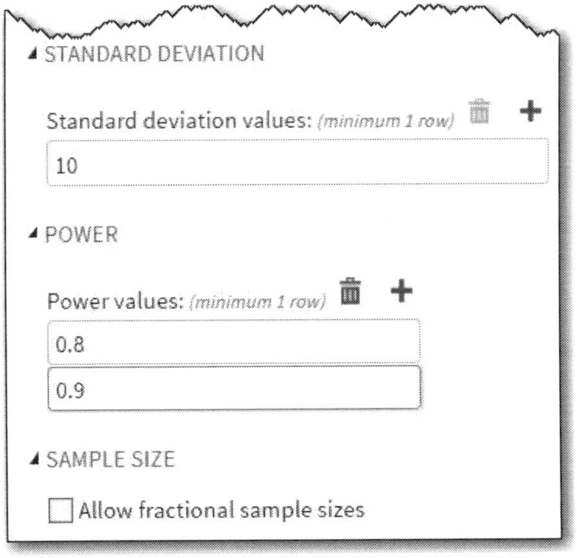

STANDARD DEVIATION

Standard deviation values: *(minimum 1 row)*

10

POWER

Power values: *(minimum 1 row)*

0.8

0.9

SAMPLE SIZE

☐ Allow fractional sample sizes

Before you run the task, click the Plots tab and make sure that the box Power by sample size plot is checked. You can let the task scale the power axis or you can specify minimum and maximum powers by checking the two boxes under Range of values (Figure 8):

Figure 8: Requesting a Plot of Power by Sample Size

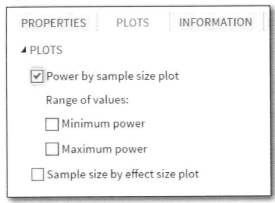

PROPERTIES   PLOTS   INFORMATION

PLOTS

☑ Power by sample size plot

Range of values:

☐ Minimum power

☐ Maximum power

☐ Sample size by effect size plot

You are ready to run the task. Figure 9 shows the results in table form, and Figure 10 shows the results in graphical form.

Figure 9: Sample Size per Group in Table Form

			Computed N per Group		
Index	Mean1	Mean2	Nominal Power	Actual Power	N per Group
1	130	120	0.8	0.807	17
2	130	120	0.9	0.912	23
3	130	125	0.8	0.801	64
4	130	125	0.9	0.903	86

Notice the large sample sizes necessary to detect a small difference of 5 points. The lowest sample size per group (n per group = 17) is for the largest difference (130 versus 120) and the lowest power (80%).

The graph of sample size by power will contain a line for each combination of means, standard deviations, and powers that you entered. The final decision of sample size is sometimes a compromise between how many subjects you can recruit (and pay for) and how large a difference you would like to be able to detect.

Figure 10: Plot of Power versus Sample Size

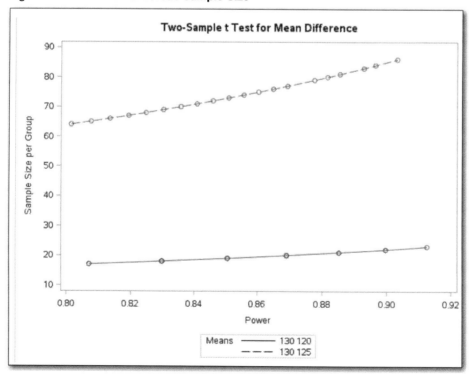

Calculating the Sample Size for a Test of Proportions

What information do you need to compute sample sizes for test of proportions? The decisions for this calculation are simpler than the decisions that you made for comparing means. The reason is that once you select a proportion, the standard deviation can be computed.

The information that you need to perform this calculation is listed below:

- Is the test to be conducted as a one-sided or two-sided test? (Usually two-sided)

- What is your alpha level? (Usually $\alpha = .05$)

- What is the proportion in the first group (usually a control group)? If unsure, lean toward .5 (maximum variance)

- How large a difference in proportions do you want to be able to detect? (Or the proportion in group two)

- What power do you want? (You often enter several values such as .8, .85, and .9)

You are now ready to run the Test of proportions task. Double-click this selection in the Power and Sample Size menu to bring up the following screen (as before, the Properties screen is shown in pieces):

Figure 11: Select Type of Test and Solve for Power or Sample Size

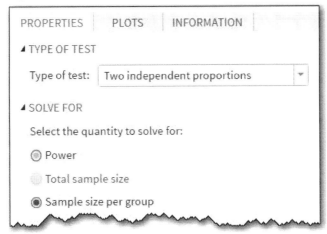

For the selection "Type of Test," select Two independent proportions. Next, decide if you want to test for power or sample size. In most cases, you will want to know how many subjects you need to obtain a desired power. You have a choice of calculating total sample size or sample size per group. Here, you chose sample size per group.

The next part of the Properties screen asks you to select the statistical test that you plan to use in the analysis. For most studies, especially with fairly large n's, the Pearson chi-square test is a good choice. If you believe that you will have small expected values in the study, you may choose Fisher's exact test. Finally, indicate if the test is to be conducted as a one-sided or two-sided test. In Figure 12, you see selections for a Pearson chi-square test conducted as a two-sided test.

Figure 12: Choose the Statistical Method That You Will Be Using

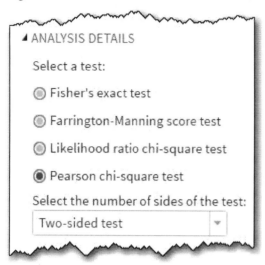

Moving farther down the menu, you see a choice for alpha (the default value of .05 is already entered) and whether you want to enter group proportions or other ways of comparing proportions such as odds ratios or relative risk. The choices in Figure 13 are alpha = .05 and Group proportions. As with the previous calculation where you were comparing means, you can also enter several choices for proportions in the two groups. You decide to compute sample sizes for two different scenarios: one with proportions of .7 and .8, the other with proportions of .7 and .9.

Figure 13: Select Alpha Level and Proportions in the Two Groups

The last entry in the properties tab is to enter one or more values for power. In Figure 14, powers of .8, .85, and .9 were selected.

Figure 14: Select One or More Power Values

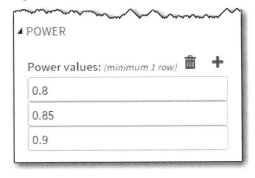

Before you run the task, click the Plots tab to request a plot of power by sample size.

Figure 15: Select Plot

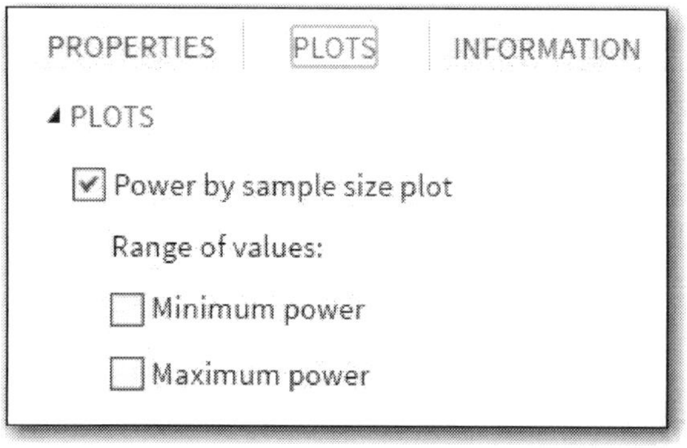

PROPERTIES | PLOTS | INFORMATION

◢ PLOTS

☑ Power by sample size plot

Range of values:

☐ Minimum power

☐ Maximum power

It's time to run the task. Click the Run icon to obtain the table and graph displayed in Figure 16 and Figure 17.

Many researchers are shocked when they see the large sample sizes needed to compare proportions. If you look at the N per Group for comparing proportions of .7 and .8 with a power of 90%, you see that you need 392 subjects per group. The smallest number of subjects per group (62) is for proportions of .7 versus .9 with 80% power.

Figure 16: Table of Results

Computed N per Group					
Index	Proportion1	Proportion2	Nominal Power	Actual Power	N per Group
1	0.7	0.8	0.80	0.801	294
2	0.7	0.8	0.85	0.851	336
3	0.7	0.8	0.90	0.900	392
4	0.7	0.9	0.80	0.803	62
5	0.7	0.9	0.85	0.854	71
6	0.7	0.9	0.90	0.900	82

You may find it more instructive to examine the sample size calculations in graphical form. As with the previous situation where you were comparing means, when you compare proportions, you may have to lower your expectations of detecting small differences and design the study with larger differences in the two proportions and, perhaps, slightly lower power.

Figure 17: Graph of Results

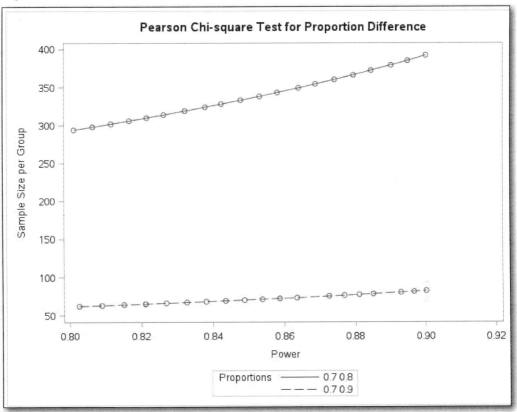

Computing Sample Size for a One-Way ANOVA Design

In the current version of SAS Studio, sample size calculations for ANOVA designs are not included in the Power and Sample size task, but they are planned for future releases. If your version of SAS Studio does not include power calculations for ANOVA designs, you can fall back on the "old way" of doing these calculations. That is, run PROC POWER, using the keyword ONEWAYANOVA along with your choices of group means, standard deviations, and power.

The program in Figure 18 computes sample size for a one-way ANOVA design, and you can use this example to help you run PROC POWER for any other one-way design.

In this example, you have made the following decisions:

- There are 3 means estimated to be 20, 25, and 30.

- You have two estimates for standard deviation: 8 and 10

- You want to compute sample size for powers of 80% and 90%.

- You want to compute the n-per-group (as compared to power for a given sample size).

- You would like a plot of Power (x-axis) versus sample size and the axes scaled to show powers from .7 to .9.

Figure 18: Using PROC POWER to Compute Power in an ANOVA Design

```
title "Computing the Power for an ANOVA Model";

proc power;
   onewayanova
   groupmeans = 20 | 25 | 30
   stddev = 8 10
   power = .80 .90
   npergroup = .;
   plot x = power min = .70 max = .90;
run;
```

You enter the group means following the key word GROUPMEANS, separating them using a vertical bar (also called a pipe symbol). Follow the keyword STDDEV with one or more estimates of the pooled standard deviation.

You have a choice of computing power or sample size. If you want to compute sample size, enter one or more values for your desired power, and enter a SAS numeric missing value (coded as a period) for the number of subjects per group. If you want to compute power for a given sample size, enter a period for the power and one or more values of sample size.

Use a PLOT statement to indicate that you want power on the x axis, with values of power ranging from .7 to .9. It is time to run the procedure.

The table and graphical output from this procedure are shown in the final two figures:

Figure 19: Table of N per Group for ANOVA Design

Computed N per Group				
Index	Std Dev	Nominal Power	Actual Power	N per Group
1	8	0.8	0.820	14
2	8	0.9	0.913	18
3	10	0.8	0.815	21
4	10	0.9	0.908	27

Figure 20: Graphical Display of Sample Size Calculations

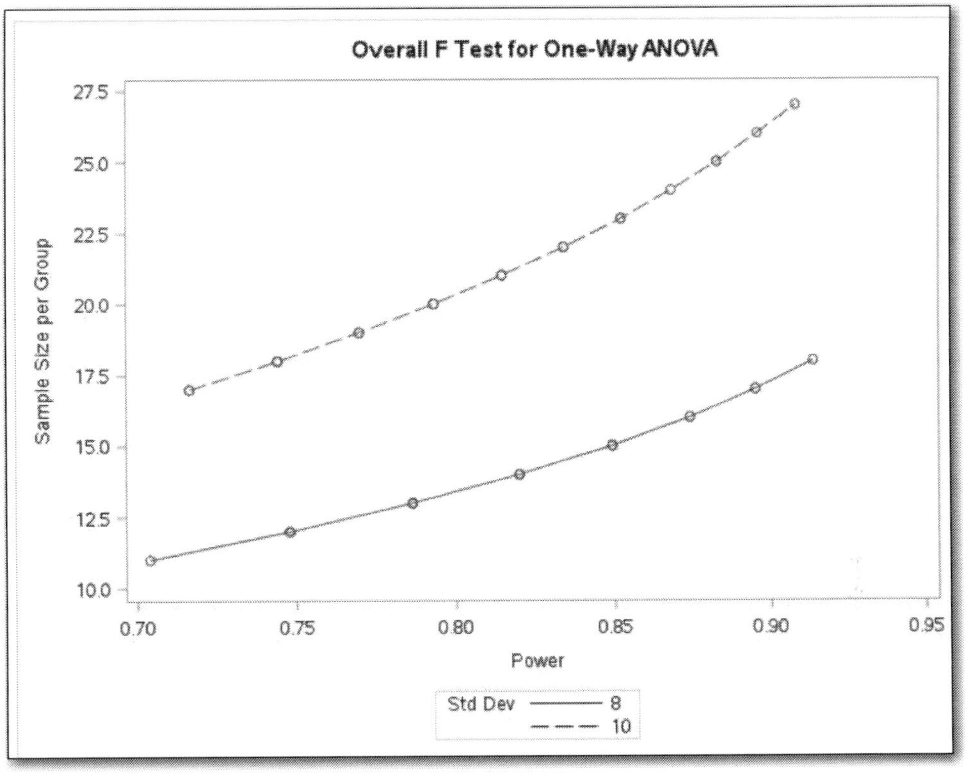

Conclusions

The SAS Studio statistics tasks include power and sample size calculations for several statistical tests, such as comparing means or comparing proportions. By seeing how to enter data for the two scenarios in this chapter, you should be able to perform calculations for the other designs in the Power and Sample size menu.

Problems

14-1: Compute the sample size per group for the following study:

Two-sample *t* test.
Two-tailed
Alpha = .05
Mean of group 1: 50
Mean of group 2: 60
Estimated pooled standard deviation: 10
Powers: 80% and 90%

14-2: Compute the sample size per group for the following study:

Two-sample *t* test.
Two-tailed
Alpha = .05
Mean of group 1: 50
Mean of group 2: 65
Estimated pooled standard deviations: 12 and 15
Powers: 80% and 90%

14-3: Compute the sample size per group for the following study:

ANOVA
Two-tailed
Alpha = .05
Mean of group 1: 50
Mean of group 2: 60
Mean of group 3: 70
Estimated pooled standard deviation: 10
Powers: 80% and 90%

14-4: Compute the sample size per group for the following study:

ANOVA
Two-tailed
Alpha = .05
Mean of group 1: 50
Mean of group 2: 60
Mean of group 3: 65
Estimated pooled standard deviation: 8
Power: 90%

14-5: Compute the sample size per group for the following study:

Test of two proportions
Two-tailed
Alpha = .05
p1 = .7
p2 = .8
Powers: 80% and 90%

14-6: Compute the sample size per group for the following study:

Test of two proportions
Two-tailed
Alpha = .05
p1 = .5
p2 = .75
Power: 80%

Instructions for Problem Sets

How to Use the Problem Set Data Files

Starting with Chapter 3, each chapter in this book contains problem sets. For some of these problems, you will need access to data. Some of the data is stored in Excel files, CSV files, raw data files, and SAS data sets.

To keep things simple, all of the data related to the end-of-chapter problems was put in a ZIP file that you can download from the site:

support.sas.com/cody

Click "Example Code and Data" under *Biostatistics by Example*, and you will see two ZIP files. One contains data files used in the book, in case you want to try running the tasks and programs yourself. The other file, labeled Problem Data, contains all of the data related to the problem sets.

The easiest way to proceed is to unzip the problem files and copy them to your hard drive to a folder called:

c:\SASUniversityEdition\myfolders\Problems

If you do this, when you open SAS Studio (assuming you set up the shared folder in the installation instructions), you will see the files in SAS Studio under My Folders and Problems. It should look something like this:

Figure 1: The Data for Problem Sets in SAS Studio

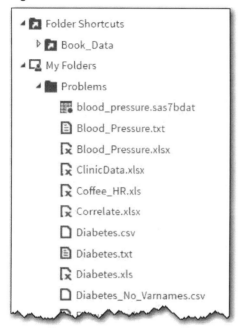

One of the data sets is a SAS data set (Blood_Pressure.sas7bdat, seen at the top of the list in Figure 1). The others are Excel files, CSV files, and text files. To use the Blood_Pressure SAS data set, you will need to create a SAS library. See the next section on how to do this.

How to Create a SAS Library

In order to use the downloaded SAS data set in any of the statistics tasks, you first need to create a SAS library. This is very easy to do—just proceed with the following steps:

1. First, expand Server Files and Folders in the Navigation pane.

2. Next, right-click "Problems" under My Folders. It should look like this:

Figure 2: Creating a SAS Library

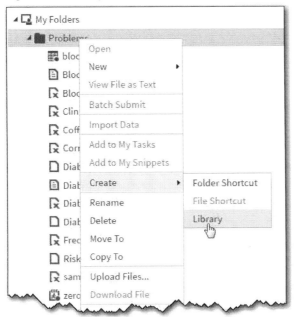

3. Select Create ▶ Library and click the left mouse button. You will see the following:

Figure 3: Next Step in Creating your SAS Library

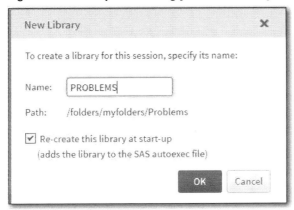

4. Enter the name PROBLEMS and check the box labeled Re-create this library at start-up.

Now, when you open a task, the PROBLEMS library will show up (see Figure 4):

Figure 4: The New PROBLEMS Library Is Now Available

Note: Your list might contain other data sets along with Blood_Pressure.

Using a SAS Data Set in the PROBLEMS Library

As an example, suppose you want to compute summary statistics on the variables SBP and DBP (systolic and diastolic blood pressures) in the Blood_Pressure SAS data set. First, select Summary Statistics in the Statistics task list. On the Data tab, click the Select a Table icon (Figure 5):

Figure 5: Select a Table

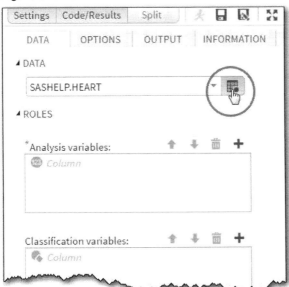

The list of tables will now show all of the SAS data sets you downloaded (Figure 6):

Figure 6: List of Tables

You can now compute summary statistics for SBP and DBP in the Blood_Pressure data set.

Figure 7: Selecting Variables from the Blood_Pressure Data Set

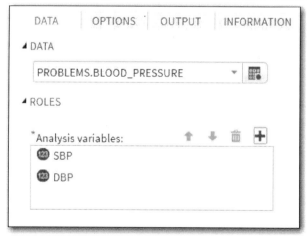

You are done!

Appendix: Solutions to the Odd-Numbered Problems

3-1: Select Tasks and utilities ▶ Utilities ▶ Import Data.

Click Select data and find the file ClinicData.xlsx. Click Change and name the work data set Clinic. Run the task. When finished, select Tasks and Utilities ▶ Data ▶ List Data.

On the Data tab, select the data set WORK.Clinic. In the List Variables box, click the plus sign and select all the variables. Run the task.

3-3: Select Tasks and Utilities ▶ Utilities ▶ Import data.

Click Select data and find the file Diabetes.csv. Click Change to change the name of the output data set to Diabetes.

Next, select Tasks and Utilities ▶ Data ▶ List Data.

On the Data tab, select the data set WORK.Diabetes. In the List Variables box, click the plus sign and select all the variables. On the Options tab, use the menu labeled Rows to list and select First n rows. Enter n = 5. Run the task.

4-1:
```
*4-1;
data Diabetes;
   Length Insulin $ 1 Diet_Drinks $ 9;
   Infile
'/folders/myfolders/problems/Diabetes_No_Varnames.csv' DSD;
   input Subj Insulin $ Diet_Drinks $ Glucose;
   *Note: Dollar signs in the INPUT statement are not
    needed because the LENGTH statement already identified
    the variables Insulin and Diet_Dinks as character.  Fine
    to leave them in the INPUT statement;
run;

title "First 5 Observations from Diabetes";
proc print data=Diabetes(obs=5);
run;
```

4-3:

```
*4-3;
data Blood_Pressure;
    infile '/folders/myfolders/problems/Blood_Pressure.txt'
dlm='09'x
    dsd pad;
    length Drug $ 7 Gender $ 1;
    input Drug Subj Gender SBP DBP;
run;
```

Select Tasks and Utilities ▶ Data ▶ List Data.

On the Data tab, select the data set WORK.Blood_Pressure. In the List Variables box, click the plus sign and select all the variables. On the Options tab, use the menu labeled Rows to list and select First n rows. Enter n = 10. Run the task.

5-1: Select Tasks and Utilities ▶ Statistics ▶ Summary.

Select SASHELP.BMT, click the Options tab, check Number of missing values and median, and uncheck minimum and maximum. Click Plots and select Histograms and Box plot.

5-3: Use the Import utility to import the workbook. Select Tasks and Utilities ▶ Statistics ▶ Distribution analysis. On the Options tab, check histogram, goodness of fit tests, and a Q-Q plot. The results of the K-S test for SBP (p=.111) and for DBP (p=.041).

5-5: Select Tasks and Utilities ▶ Statistics ▶ One-way frequencies. On the Options tab, expand Plots and check Suppress plots. Also on the Options tab, check Omit cumulative frequencies.

6-1: Select Tasks and Utilities ▶ Import data. Select Diabetes.xls and name your output data set Diabetes.

Select Tasks and Utilities ▶ Statistics ▶ t tests. Select a one-sample test and select Glucose as the analysis variable. On the Options tab, check Tests for normality and nonparametric tests. All tests fail to reject the null hypothesis, and the tests for normality also fail to reject the null hypothesis that the glucose values are normally distributed.

6-3: Select Tasks and Utilities ▶ Statistics ▶ t tests. Next, on the Data tab, select the SASHELP.Heart data set. Check tests for normality and default plots on the Options tab as well as the alternate hypothesis that the mean is not equal to 150. The surprisingly low *p*-value results from the very large sample size (over 5,000), which gives the test very high power to detect even small differences.

7-1: Select Tasks and Utilities ▶ Statistics ▶ t tests. On the Data tab, select the Diabetes data set. Also on the Data tab, click Filter and enter the line:

```
Diet_Drinks ne 'Sometimes'
```

When you run the two-sample *t* test with Glucose as the Analysis variable and Diet_Drinks as the Groups variable, you will see a highly significant result (t = 4.94, p<.0001), with the

Glucose mean higher in the Diet_Drinks group = 'Often' compared to 'Rarely'. This data set is fictitious, but there may be some evidence that diet drinks can raise blood glucose levels.

7-3: Data Step approach.

```
data Coffee;
    input Subj Before After;
datalines;
1        75        83
2        65        86
3        69        68
4        65        54
5        68        60
6        77        64
7        76        67
8        74        70
9        85        53
10       63        87
11       71        90
12       62        59
;
```

Then select Tasks and Utilities ▶ Statistics ▶ t tests. Select Paired t test. Enter After as the Group 1 variable and Before as the Group 2 variable. p=.0428 and you do not reject the null hypothesis that the data values are normally distributed.

8-1: Use the Import utility to create a SAS data set from the Blood_Pressure.xls workbook. Next bring up the one-way tab: Select Tasks and Utilities ▶ One-way ANOVA.

On the Data tab, select WORK.BP as the data set, SBP as the dependent variable, and Drug as the categorical variable. You can accept all the default values on the Options tab. The resulting *p*-value for the ANOVA is .0197. The Tukey multiple comparison tests shows that Placebo and Drug B are significantly different (p = .0077). Even though Levene's test for homogeneity of variance is significant, the variances are close enough to run the test. Remember that this assumption can be violated a bit, especially when the number of subjects per group is equal (as in this case) or nearly equal.

8-3: Import the Diabetes.xls workbook in the usual way. Next start the One-way ANOVA task: Select Tasks and Utilities ▶ Statistics ▶ One-Way ANOVA. Select WORK.Diabetes on the Data tab and accept all the defaults on the Options tab. The Overall *p*-value is <.0001. The Tukey multiple comparison test shows a significant difference between Often and Rarely (p = <.0001) and a nearly significant difference between Rarely and Sometimes (p = .0585).

8-5: Start out in the usual way: Select Tasks and Utilities ▶ Statistics ▶ One-Way ANOVA.

Select SASHELP.BMT on the Options tab and select T as the analysis variable and Group as the categorical variable. Overall *p*-value = .0012. Significant differences between All and Low Risk (p=.0081) and between Low Risk and High Risk (p=.0031).

9-1: Create the SAS data set BP using the Import utility. Next, run the N-way ANOVA task: Select Tasks and Utilities ▶ Statistics ▶ N-Way ANOVA.

Select WORK.BP on the Data tab, DBP as the analysis variable, and the two variables Drug and Gender as factors. Next click on the Model tab, select the two variables Drug and Gender, and then click Full factorial model. On the Options tab, choose to look at main effects; and, under plots, include Diagnostic plots. The interaction term is not significant, and only Drug is significant at the .05 level. Tukey comparisons show that there is a difference between Drug A and Placebo (p = .0137).

9-3: Use the Import facility to create the Diabetes dataset. Next, select Tasks and Utilities ▶ Statistics ▶ N-Way ANOVA.

On the Data tab, select WORK.Diabetes. Select Glucose as the dependent variable with Diet_Drinks and Insulin as factors. Click Model and Edit. Select Diet_Drinks and Insulin and then Full Factorial model. On the Options tab, in the list under Select statistics, choose All effects. You will see a significant interaction term in the model. To determine pairwise differences, you need to look at the *p*-values for each combination of Diet_Drinks and Insulin.

9-5: Run the SAS program shown in the problem (or enter the data in an Excel workbook and import it). Next, select Tasks and Utilities ▶ Statistics ▶ N-Way ANOVA.

On the Data tab, select WORK.CHF. Choose LVEF as the dependent variable with Group and Weight as the two factors. On the Model tab, select the two variables, and click Full factorial model. On the options tab, select a Tukey multiple comparison test. The overall *p*-value for the model is .0258. The *p*-values for Group, Weight, and the interaction are .0094, .3708, and .2033 respectively. The Tukey multiple comparison test shows Calcium to be different from Lasix and Calcium to be different from Placebo.

10-1: Create the data set BP using the Import task on the Utilities menu. Next, select Tasks and Utilities ▶ Statistics ▶ Correlation analysis.

On the Options tab, in the Display statistics menu, select Selected statistics. Then click Spearman's Rank Order Correlations. Under Plots, select Individual plots.

10-3: SelectTasks and Utilities ▶ Data ▶ Select Random Sample.

On the Data tab, select SASHELP.Heart. On the Options tab, name the output data set Sample_Heart. On the Options tab, choose the sampling method Without replacement. Set the number in the sample to 500, and click the box to specify the random seed. Enter the number 13579 in the box provided. Next run the Correlation Analysis task on the Statistics menu, using the WORK.Sample_Heart data set that you just created. Select the three variables Height, Weight, and Cholesterol. On the Options tab, be sure to check *p*-values on the selected statistics menu. Request a matrix of scatter plots.

Comparing the correlations and p-values, notice that the correlations are similar to the ones you obtained with the full data set but the p-values are much larger.

10-5: Run the original program:

```
data Outlier;
   input X Y @@;
datalines;
0 2 5 6 6 2 3 3 1 3 4 4 8 1 6 4 2 5 4 2 6 5
;
```

and the program with the added data point:

```
data Outlier;
   input X Y @@;
datalines;
0 2 5 6 6 2 3 3 1 3 4 4 8 1 6 4 2 5 4 2 6 5 15 15
;
```

The correlation coefficient without the extra data point is .03586 (p = .9166). With the added data point, the Pearson correlation is .72767 (p = .00373), and the Spearman Correlation is .19464 (p = .5444). The lesson is to always produce a scatter plot of the data and look for outliers.

11-1: Select Tasks and Utilities ▶ Statistics ▶ Linear Regression.

On the Data tab, select SASHELP.Heart, Weight as the dependent variable, and Height as a Continuous variable. The predicted weight for a person 65 inches tall is 153.86 pounds.

11-3: Select SASHELP.Heart on the Data tab, Weight as the dependent variable, Sex as the classification variable, and Cholesterol, Systolic, and Diastolic as continuous variables. Edit the model in the usual way. Run the model. Rerun the model with Stepwise selection selected on the Selection method tab. Only two variables, Sex and Diastolic, enter using the stepwise technique.

12-1: Select Tasks and Utilities ▶ Statistics ▶ Binary Logistic regression. Select SASHELP.Heart on the Data tab and click Filter.

Enter the clause:

```
BP_Status ne 'Optimal'
```

Next, select Status as the Response variable and 'Dead' as the event of interest. Select Chol_Status and BP_Status as Classification variables. Under parameterization of effects, choose Reference coding.

12-3: Use the import utility to create the data set Risk (don't forget to click the Change button to change the default name IMPORT to Risk). Next select Tasks and Utilities ▶ Statistics ▶ Binary logistic regression.

On the Data tab, select the WORK.Risk data set and the two variables Chol_High and Age_Group as Classification variables. Click on parameterization and select reference coding. On the Model tab, select the two variables Chol_High and Age_Group. Then click Add.

13-1: Create the Risk data set using the Import Utility. Next, select Tasks and Utilities ▶ Statistics ▶ One-Way Frequencies.

> Select the data set WORK.Risk on the Data tab and highlight the variables Age_Group, Chol_High, Gender, and Heart_Attack. On the Options tab, click Plots and check the box to suppress plots. Also on the Options tab, uncheck the option to compute cumulative frequencies and percentages.

13-3: This solution uses a slightly different technique than discussed in this chapter. You may choose to make a new, temporary SAS data set with assigned formats or use the solution presented here that adds a FORMAT statement as part of PROC FORMAT. When you include a FORMAT statement in a PROC, the association between the variables and formats exists only for that procedure—when you include a FORMAT statement in a DATA step, the association remains for any procedure using that data set. Here is what the edited task code should look like:

```
proc format;
    value yesno 1 = '1:Yes'
                0 = '2:No';
run;

proc freq data=WORK.RISK order=formatted;
    format Chol_High Heart_Attack yesno.;
    tables  (Chol_High) *(Heart_Attack) / chisq relrisk
nopercent nocum plots=none;
run;
```

> Remember to add the option ORDER=formatted in PROC FREQ.

13-5: Create an Excel workbook that looks like this:

Outcome	Risk_Factor	Count
Bad	1-Yes	5
Good	1-Yes	3
Bad	2-No	2
Bad	2-No	15

> Convert this workbook to a SAS data set using the Import utility. Next, go to the Statistics task Table Analysis. Choose the newly created SAS data set and choose Outcome as the row variable and Risk_Factor as the column variable. Under Additional tasks, select Count as the frequency variable. On the Options tab, check chi-square. The Fisher's exact test (2-tailed) value is .0169, and the continuity corrected chi-square p-value is .0309.

14-1: For a power of 80%, n per group = 17. For a power of 90%, n per group is 23.

14-3: Submit the following SAS program:

```
proc power;
   onewayanova
   groupmeans = 50 | 60 | 70
   stddev = 10
   power = .80 .90
   npergroup = .;
   plot x = power min = .70 max = .90;
run;
```

For a power of 80%, the n per group = 6. For a power of 90%, the n per group = 8.

14-5: For a power of 80%, the n per group = 294. For a power of 90%, the n per group = 392

Index

W

X

Y

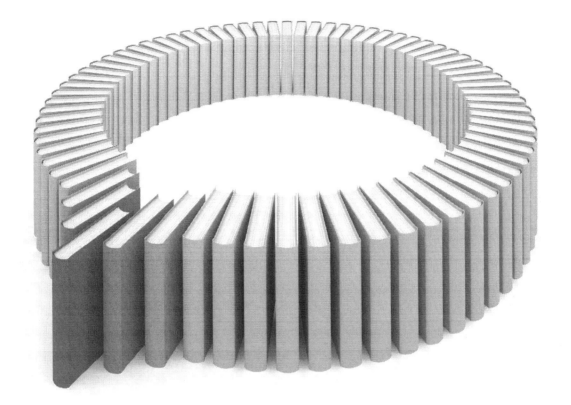

Gain Greater Insight into Your SAS® Software with SAS Books.

Discover all that you need on your journey to knowledge and empowerment.

support.sas.com/bookstore
for additional books and resources.

THE POWER TO KNOW®

SAS and all other SAS Institute Inc. product or service names are registered trademarks or trademarks of SAS Institute Inc. in the USA and other countries. ® indicates USA registration. Other brand and product names are trademarks of their respective companies. © 2013 SAS Institute Inc. All rights reserved. S107969US.0413